CHURCH GROWTH

Very few young leaders at the dawn of this new millennium have Wayne Cordeiro's combination of gifts, character and leadership. I am completely unreserved in recommending his work because I know him well. I trust his vision and values in both a personal and public dimension, and I believe he is being raised up by God as a voice to the larger Body at this pivotal time in the Church.

JACK W. HAYFORD
FOUNDING PASTOR, THE CHURCH ON THE WAY
CHANCELLOR, THE KING'S COLLEGE AND SEMINARY
VAN NUYS, CALIFORNIA

By definition, leaders build teams, and Wayne Cordeiro is one of the best team-building leaders I've ever known. I suggest you visit New Hope Fellowship in Hawaii and witness firsthand just how thrilling ministry can be when the right people are serving in the right places, shoulder to shoulder with others who love serving Christ together. Read this book slowly and absorb its contents fully. You will discover there is no limit to what God can do through a church that does its ministry as a team.

BILL HYBELS
SENIOR PASTOR, WILLOW CREEK COMMUNITY CHURCH
SOUTH BARRINGTON, ILLINOIS

A joyous book written in the breezy style of a native island song, *Doing Church as a Team* isn't just about mobilizing people to do the work of the church. This is about releasing people into a whole new spiritual dimension in their lives—a place where they begin to understand that God created each of us for a purpose. Mahalo, Wayne!

JOHN C. MAXWELL
FOUNDER, THE INJOY GROUP
ATLANTA, GEORGIA

Wayne Cordeiro's thriving congregation is one of America's truly great churches. *Doing Church as a Team*, however, is not about how to build a megachurch. Wayne is committed to building people one by one. His passion is to help every believer find his or her unique place of fruitful service in God's house and among the lost in God's harvest fields.

RON MEHL
PASTOR, BEAVERTON FOURSQUARE CHURCH
BEAVERTON, OREGON

The key word in this book is "team." Wayne Cordeiro is equipping people for leadership and giving them a vision of how to pull together to build the work of God. The principles in this book will work in a church of fifty as well as they do in Pastor Cordeiro's megachurch in Honolulu.

ELMER L. TOWNS
DEAN OF THE SCHOOL OF RELIGION, LIBERTY UNIVERSITY
LYNCHBURG, VIRGINIA

There is no such thing as a formula for growing a church, but there are foundational principles underlying the growth of every one. Wayne Cordeiro has these principles in place, and he shares his secrets in this remarkable book.

C. PETER WAGNER
CHANCELLOR, WAGNER LEADERSHIP INSTITUTE
COLORADO SPRINGS, COLORADO

DOING CHURCH
—AS A—
TEAM

WAYNE CORDEIRO

Regal

A Division of Gospel Light
Ventura, California, U.S.A.

Published by Regal Books
A Division of Gospel Light
Ventura, California, U.S.A.
Printed in the U.S.A.

Regal Books is a ministry of Gospel Light, an evangelical Christian publisher dedicated to serving the local church. We believe God's vision for Gospel Light is to provide church leaders with biblical, user-friendly materials that will help them evangelize, disciple and minister to children, youth and families.

It is our prayer that this Regal book will help you discover biblical truth for your own life and help you meet the needs of others. May God richly bless you.

For a free catalog of resources from Regal Books/Gospel Light, please call your Christian supplier or contact us at 1-800-4-GOSPEL or www.regalbooks.com.

Revised and expanded edition. *Doing Church as a Team* was originally published by New Hope Publishers, Honolulu, Hawaii, in 1998.

Published in association with the literary agency of Alive Communications, Inc., 7680 Goddard Street, Suite 200, Colorado Springs, Colorado 80920.

Cover and Interior Design by Robert Williams
Revised edition edited by David Webb

LIBRARY OF CONGRESS CATALOGING-IN-PUBLICATION DATA
Cordeiro, Wayne.
      Doing church as a team / Wayne Cordeiro.— Rev. ed.
            p.   cm.
      Includes bibliographical references.
      ISBN 0-8307-2666-7 (hc) — ISBN 0-8307-2652-7 (pbk.)
      1. Church work.

      BV4400 .C66   2001
      259—dc21   00-045754

1 2 3 4 5 6 7 8 9 10 11 12 13 14 15 / 05 04 03 02 01 00

Rights for publishing this book in other languages are contracted by Gospel Literature International (GLINT). GLINT also provides technical help for the adaptation, translation and publishing of Bible study resources and books in scores of languages worldwide. For further information, write to GLINT, P.O. Box 4060, Ontario, CA 91761-1003, U.S.A. You may also send e-mail to Glintint@aol.com, or visit the GLINT website at www.glint.org.

CONTENTS

ACKNOWLEDGMENTS

I want to say *mahalo* (Hawaiian for "thank you") to the many people who have given me input and inspiration for this book. Whether they realized it or not, I have been mentored by scores of wonderful people who may never win a prize or get their names in print. These are my silent heroes, people who have jewel-studded crowns awaiting them from the One whom they serve so willingly.

Thank you to the many who have taught me along the way:

To the wonderful New Hope Churches in the Pacific Rim. You are my family.

To Clarke Bright, Randy Furushima, Elwin Ahu, Mike Lwin, Creighton Daniel Arita and Guy Higashi, for making it all come together. Thank you for always reaching for God's best and never saying that it couldn't be done! I asked you to reach high, and you touched the heavens with your heart's response. I have learned so much as we've partnered together. What a ride!

To David Webb and Dawn O'Brien, for your alchemy with words and how you took my stilted thoughts and gave them life.

To Eva and Bertram, Linda DeCosta, the Iranons and the Takakis, for your dear friendship.

To Steve and Cindy Kenny, Dane Ison, the Tiltons and all the wonderful artists, dancers and musicians of New Hope's Front Lines, for your partnership in redeeming the arts.

To our fantastic "Levites" ministry, for following the pillar so willingly through the setting up and taking down of our worship facilities every Sunday!

To all the wonderful volunteer teams too numerous to mention: Hospitality, 1st Impressions, Mercy Ministries, Children's Ministries and dozens more. Thank you for who you are. You always remind me how beautiful is the Body of Christ!

To Mary Hiyama and Doris Aoki, for consistently showing me what being a servant is all about.

To Pauline Spencer, for keeping Jeannie in line; and to the staff in Hilo, for always believing.

To Jon Yamazaki, for our many travels to Japan as a team, and to Alex Pacheco, for the memories of learning at sea about God's call on our lives.

To the many others who have shaped my life: the late Dr. Roy Hicks, Jr., Bill Hybels of Willow Creek Community Church, Bruce Bugbee, Bill Gothard and Rick Warren of Saddleback Community Church. Thank you especially to Dr. Paul Risser, who taught me so many things about developing people skills. You have been a great mentor to me over the years.

To Noel Campbell, for serving tirelessly with me when I began to pioneer churches, and to my dear friends Dan and Carol Ann Shima, who put their hands to the plow and never looked back.

To all the wonderful staff and leaders at New Hope Christian Fellowship in Oahu, for graciously allowing me to paddle with them.

To my dear wife, Anna, and my children Amy, Aaron and Abigail, from whom I have learned so much. I have so much yet to learn, but with your love and support, I will never give up! Each one of you is a gift to my life and to the whole Church!

REACHING FOR GOD'S BEST

D OING CHURCH AS A TEAM IS NOT AN INNOVA-TIVE CONCEPT. INSTEAD, IT IS AS OLD AS THE BIBLE ITSELF BUT, HOPEFULLY, DESCRIBED HERE IN CONTEMPORARY TERMS. ECCLESIASTES 1:9 TELLS US THAT THERE IS NOTHING NEW UNDER THE SUN. WE GET TO LEARN FROM EACH OTHER. RICK WARREN, PASTOR OF SADDLEBACK COMMUNITY CHURCH IN CALIFORNIA, ONCE QUIPPED, "I OFFERED A MAN AN IDEA TO TRY, BUT HE DECLINED AND TOLD ME IN NO UNCERTAIN TERMS THAT HE WAS GOING TO EITHER BE ORIGINAL OR NOTHING . . . SO HE BECAME BOTH."

It is my deep desire that this book will help leaders put an age-old concept into action. The ideas herein are more than just the accumulation of 25 years in ministry. I have included lessons learned from making hundreds of mistakes as well as gems gleaned from observing many wonderful churches and leaders in action. This approach to doing church is the very heart and passion of an amazing church in Honolulu called New Hope Christian Fellowship of Oahu—our tenth pioneer work since 1984. After five years, the average attendance on Sunday mornings has grown to more than 7,000. Of that number, more than 5,200 have made first-time commitments to follow Christ, and more than 4,000 of those have been baptized.

The church outgrew me in its first month. If it weren't for the outstanding servants whom God brought to serve there, I am sure I would be locked away in the mental ward of a state institution by now. (Perhaps some feel I should enroll anyway!) Because of our accelerated growth, doing church as a team was almost a necessity. Although I had been in ministry for more than two decades, I was more certain than ever that I knew much less than I thought I did. Yet through all the trials and struggles, a diamond was formed and a gem was fashioned. My heart's desire is to deposit the truths I learned here into your account!

This book is written for both pastors and members of congregations who have a deep desire to make a difference with their lives. I pray you'll come away motivated and inspired in your walk with the Lord, encouraged to keep reaching for God's very best. It is written for leaders who, like myself, have found the status quo to be unacceptable. At times I will address my comments to pastors and, at other times, to volunteer leaders.

But in the final analysis, these truths apply to every person and every church in every denomination. This isn't a book on how to make your church more like our church or how to adopt another church's style. Instead, it is a book on how to become more like the person or church Jesus created you to be. We must learn from each other, and if we do, we'll be miles farther toward becoming all God desires for us!

I have often wrestled with the fact that if the Word of God indeed is powerful, then why does the average church in America have fewer than 100 people in attendance every Sunday morning? And although violent crime has declined, the prison population in America has dramatically risen by 500 percent since 1975.[1] With more than 300,000 churches in the United States, we can do better. I know we can. And if we join hearts and hands and learn from each other, we can bring this country back from the brink!

DESIGNED FOR EACH OTHER

God would never have given us the Great Commission to go into all the world and preach the gospel if He never intended for that to really happen. Peter tells us that the Lord is not willing "for any to perish but for all to come to repentance" (2 Pet. 3:9). God would not say it if it were not possible. But none of us can do it alone. No pastor can singlehandedly fulfill that calling, regardless of how gifted he may be. Unless every one of us catches the fire, in the long run there will be no warmth against the chill of the age we're living in.

Jigoro Kano was the founder of the art of judo and the highest-ranking black belt in this world-renowned sport. Nearing his death, Kano made one last request of his students. He asked that they bury him wearing a white belt, the symbol of a beginner, a learner. My prayer is that we will always be learners. In fact, the Greek word for "disciple," *mathetes*, comes from the verb *manthano*, meaning "to learn." Humility and teachability are the crown jewels of all the qualities of a leader whom God will use in this new century.

May we learn God's design for His people and begin to respect and appreciate each other's giftings. There are few things more beautiful to God than seeing His people serving and working together in a united rhythm. It's like a symphony to His ears. That's how we were created to function. God has designed us to need each other! For us to reach our communities, much less the world, we will need every ministry doing its part and every congregation excitedly doing church as a team.

My dear friend Tom Paterson described it in this way: "If I have one good idea, and you have one good idea, how many ideas does each of us have? The answer? One." He continued, "Now if I share my idea with you and you share yours with me, how many does each one *now* have? Answer? *Two!* You see," he went on, a gleam in his eye, "if we share our ideas with each other, we have doubled our knowledge immediately! Have you lost your own idea? No! You still have it. But by sharing, we have increased our knowledge 100 percent."

I am learning that I cannot be fulfilled apart from other people. In fact, the bottom line of this entire book is this: *You can't do it alone.* If you want to be a successful leader, if you plan to have a successful ministry, you must develop not only your gifts but also the gifts of others around you. If you give your life away, you'll end up discovering what life is all about!

JESUS' PRAYER

*That they may all be one; even as Thou, Father, art in Me,
and I in Thee, that they also may be in Us; that the world
may believe that Thou didst send Me (John 17:21).*

This was one of Jesus' final prayers for the Church before He was
betrayed and crucified. I often notice that, as Christians, we are
constantly asking God to answer our prayers. There's nothing
inherently wrong with that. He is so faithful to answer. But after
reading this verse, I thought, *Wouldn't it be nice if for once, just once,
we could answer one of HIS prayers?*

Doing church as a team is one of the ways we can do that.
That's what this book is all about. After all, He has answered
hundreds of billions of our prayers! Now maybe we can finally
answer one of His!

Note

1. Chuck Colson, "Not Out of the Woods: Why Crime Is Falling," *BreakPoint
with Chuck Colson*, broadcast February 10, 1999. Transcript is available on
the Internet at http://www.breakpoint.org.

EXPERIENCE THE RHYTHM

I N 1984, WE MOVED OUR FAMILY TO THE BIG ISLAND OF HAWAII. I HAD LIVED IN OREGON DURING MY JUNIOR HIGH SCHOOL YEARS AFTER BEING RAISED IN THE PALOLO VALLEY OF OAHU. AFTER I GRADUATED FROM BIBLE COLLEGE AND SPENT TEN YEARS IN YOUTH MINISTRY, GOD PLACED AN UNDENIABLE CALL ON MY HEART TO RETURN TO HAWAII AND SHEPHERD THE PEOPLE IN A COMMU-NITY CALLED HILO.

Nestled between the two mountains of Mauna Kea and Mauna Loa, Hilo is one of the most beautiful cities on the islands. Stretching eastward is a natural bay that welcomed some of the first missionaries to Hawaii. Lying at the foot of these two imposing mountains, which are usually topped with snow in the winter, Hilo is the recipient of constant rain showers, giving it the distinction of being the wettest city in the United States, with an average annual rainfall of more than 120 inches!

Hilo also has some of the most beautiful people in the world. They are fun-loving, relationship-oriented people with much *aloha*, or love for one another. They enjoy sports, fishing, eating, music and laughter.

One of the more popular sports on the islands is canoe paddling. In this sport, there are six paddlers in a canoe, or *wa`a*, which has a balancing arm called an *ama*. Although navigating one of these ancient canoes may look basic, the technique required is much more than meets the eye.

One summer, six of us from the church were invited to compete as a crew in an upcoming canoe race. We were game for something new, so we accepted and immediately sought out one of the canoe instructors from a nearby club for a few lessons. We started our first lesson in an adjacent lake of brackish water. Our instructor, Russell Chin, sat astride the nose of the canoe, facing us as he called out signals and instructions.

We were in our places, and the first lesson began.

"OK, everyone!" he yelled. "This is how you hold a paddle," he said, modeling the correct form. As we were figuring out which end we were to grasp and with which hand, he continued.

"We're going to paddle our first stretch of water. It will be an eighth-of-a-mile sprint. When I begin the stopwatch and say 'Go,' just paddle as fast and hard as you can. When we cross the finish line, I'll notify you. That's when you can stop paddling. Got it?"

How hard can this be? I thought. *Even women paddle canoes. This ought to be a breeze!* Just then, my self-confident thoughts were shattered by the sharp call of our coach.

"*Ho`omakaukau? I mua!*"

In English, it means, "Ready? Go forward!"

With our muscles bulging and sinews stretched, we burst out of our dead-in-the-water starting position like a drowning elephant trying to get air. We thrashed the water with our paddles on either side of the canoe. Not knowing when to switch from one side to the other, we all figured the best time would simply be when one arm got tired. So, firing at will, I crossed the blade of my oar over and across the canoe; and when I did, I scraped the back of my fellow paddler, Roy Pua-Kaipo, seated directly in front of me. He grunted as my oar etched an unmistakable red mark across his spine. But Roy didn't stop. He just kept beating the water like a trooper. We were on a crusade!

It felt as if hours had transpired. My arms became like lead, and my lungs were on fire. Roy's back was starting to bleed, and our canoe was half filled with water. The elephant was beginning to drown when we finally heard Russell yell, "OK, stop!"

Thank God! I thought. We abandoned the sinking canoe and let our bodies slump into the water, totally exhausted.

"One minute, 42 seconds," Russell called. "Pretty sad!"

Like war-torn warriors, we comforted each other, apologizing for the scrapes and wounds inflicted by our flailing paddles. We started bailing the water out of the canoe, which had begun to resemble a defeated submarine more than a sleek racing vessel.

Russell gathered us whimpering novices together, and after sharing a few basics about safety, he taught us how to paddle as a team. Each fledgling paddler was to mirror the one in front of him, and everyone was to move in time with the lead stroker. He taught us how to switch our paddles to the opposite hand without injuring each other. We practiced together again and again until our stroking became as rhythmic as a metronome. We were beginning to look good! After a few practice runs, our coach took us back to our original starting position.

"All right," said Russell, "let's try that same eighth-mile stretch again! Only this time, I want you to stroke as if you were taking a leisurely stroll through the park. No sprinting. Just mirror the one in front of you and switch with a smooth cadence of rhythm, just as you were taught! Stroke as a team and don't try to break any sound barriers this time, OK?"

With new confidence, we took our mark. Russell barked out the starting signal. *"Ho`omakaukau? I mua!"*

Our oars silently entered the water, coordinated in perfect time. Mike Diaz, the lead stroker, called out his command, "Hut!" In perfect chorus, we answered, "Ho!" and we were off.

Our canoe cut through the water like a knife through jelly. We switched sides without skipping a beat. We each mirrored the rower in front of us. We were being transformed from a drowning circus animal into a precision machine! Then just as we were feeling the exhilaration of smooth progress, Russell yelled, "OK! Stop paddling."

The ahead-of-expected arrival caught all of us by surprise.

"Anybody tired?"

We all shook our heads no!

Russell held up his stopwatch so that we could see. Then he exclaimed, "You beat your last time by 24 seconds!"

I couldn't believe it! Nobody was injured! No one went overboard out of sheer exhaustion! No canoe deluged with water! No fire in my lungs! It was a sheer delight! We congratulated each other, gave a few victory shouts, exchanged leis and took pictures. This was amazing!

And we did it together! We paddled as a team.

Just like paddling a canoe, God designed His people to stroke together for a purpose. He has designed each church with a special purpose, and His plan is to saturate the carrying out of that ministry with joy. In order for this to happen, God has given each of us a unique gift. The combination of our gifts working in synch should give off such a radiance that the whole world will stand up and take notice!

Each of us has been given a paddle by God. A gift. A calling. And like the paddlers of a canoe, each of us has a place or a role to fill. On each paddle is our unique thumbprint, our own individual circuitry, designed by God Himself. He places each of us in a community, more specifically in a local church, with a divine purpose. He fits us alongside others who have a similar assignment and calls us a family, a team, the Church. No one person is meant to carry out this assignment alone; it wasn't designed that way. We were created to do church as a team!

A full symphony under the direction of a master conductor will always sound infinitely better than a one-man band. As we discover and develop our individual gifts and learn to stroke in rhythm as a team, we will be absolutely astonished at how much further we get—and with fewer injuries!

CHAPTER ONE

GOD HAS A PLAN

You did not choose Me, but I chose you,
and appointed you, that you should go and bear fruit,
and that your fruit should remain.

JOHN 15:16

GOD DOESN'T DO THINGS AT RANDOM. LIKE GOD DID WITH JEREMIAH, HE PLANNED YOUR BIRTH BEFORE YOU WERE EVEN CONCEIVED! HE CHOSE YOU, CREATED YOU AND THEN DELICATELY PLACED YOU ON HIS SOVEREIGN TIME CONTINUUM.

God never makes mistakes. I have searched the Bible thoroughly, and I have yet to find even one instance where God said, "Oops!" Sorry, you won't find that word in any concordance.

Isn't it true that, if God wanted to, He could have created you to have been born in the tenth century? You could have been born in any of the years before Christ. But for some reason, He wanted you to be born and living now, in this century, in this day and age. He has a purpose and a plan for you!

If He wanted to, He could have had you placed in another nation. You could be living in Eastern Europe or Africa, not speaking English but Hungarian or Swahili!

Let's take this a step further. Of all the states in the United States of America, He has chosen for me to live in the one I am in now, Hawaii. (Thank God!) But have you ever located Hawaii on a globe or a map? You can hardly find the place! For many years, I thought Hawaii was located just off the tip of Alaska, because on every map I saw while growing up, Hawaii was in a small box located just off the Alaskan coastline! But still, of all the landmasses on this globe, He chose one of a tiny grouping of islands—the state of Hawaii—for me to reside on.

God also preselected the city you are living in right now. He didn't place you in just any part of the city; He placed you in the very neighborhood where you now reside! And furthermore, of all the churches He could have put you in, He has placed you in one specific church.

I think that's a miracle!

From one man he made every nation of men, that they should inhabit the whole earth; and he determined the times set for them and the exact places where they should live (Acts 17:26, NIV).

God doesn't make any mistakes. He has a plan! We find it written: "For we are His workmanship, created in Christ Jesus for good works, which God prepared beforehand, that we should walk in them" (Eph. 2:10). God prepared our paths beforehand that we should walk in them! He has a plan for each and every one of us, and it is our responsibility to find out what that plan is and then walk in it:

I chose you, and appointed you, that you should go and bear fruit, and that your fruit should remain (John 15:16).

God chose you for a very specific purpose. If God didn't have a special purpose for you and if He didn't want you to succeed, then you wouldn't have been born! He wouldn't have created you. Sometimes we read in the newspaper of those who get so depressed that they end up taking their own lives. They lost their reason to live, and suicide was the quickest escape route from their pain. Did God make some kind of cosmic mistake? Did each of these people with tragic endings really have a life empty of purpose?

God never makes mistakes. Never! And by the way, you didn't choose Him. God chose you and appointed you that you should be fruitful with your life, so don't settle for anything less. You have one life to live on this Earth. Invest it wisely. Don't squander it or misuse it!

ONLY ONE LIFE TO GIVE

This globe we're riding on called Earth is not as still as it may appear. It's traveling at more than 60,000 miles per hour! That's right. The Earth is rotating faster than the spin cycle of your washing machine. "Time flies" is more than a trite phrase. That's why the psalmists describe life to be as transient as a "breath" (Ps. 144:4), the passing of our years but a "sigh" (Ps. 90:9). James likens our life to a "vapor" that is here today and gone tomorrow (Jas. 4:14). Our life is indeed flashing before our eyes! A few more spins, and it will be over. We'll be in eternity.

The Bible tells us that Jesus paid dearly for something called eternal life that He made available to each of us. How long is eternity? Comparing life on this Earth with the eternity that Jesus purchased for us, I would describe it in this way: Imagine that you attached the end of a cable to an arrow and shot it in one direction. The cable went straight toward the horizon until the end was out of sight. Then you took the other end of the cable and shot it in the opposite direction. Let's say the cable now stretches through the room you're in and is directly in front of you. It passes through both of the walls on either side of the room and stretches unseen into the distance. Now that's what eternity is like. Eternity, like the cable, is forever extending in both directions with no end in sight.

To contrast the brevity of our earthly existence with that of eternity, I would take out my ballpoint pen and draw a vertical scratch on the extended cable. Then I would tell you that the width of that scratch mark (about 1/32 of an inch) represents how long our life on Earth is in comparison with eternity. Not very long!

But do you know what most people do? They not only live on that scratch, but they also love that scratch. They kiss the scratch. They save for that scratch. They hoard for that scratch. They live scratch lives, have scratch businesses and have scratch families with scratch hopes and scratch dreams.

But God so loved that scratch that He sent His only begotten Son to die for those who live there. Yet many still don't know about this gift called eternal life! They're still hanging on to the scratch. They try to elongate it, stretch it and extend it as much as possible. But even in the midst of their attempts, they know deep inside that there's got to be something more.

The Bible says God put eternity in the heart of every man (see Eccles. 3:11). This is why each person longs for more than what the world can offer. There is the classic quote from Blaise Pascal who said there is a God-shaped void in the heart of every man. Although many try to fill this void with material possessions or mind-altering drugs and alcohol, only God Himself can fill that aching chasm.

The fact that you are reading this is a good sign that you have heard His invitation and have chosen to follow Him. You are saved. What an amazing grace He's extended to you and me! But that's not all there is! Let me tell you . . . the rest of the story.

GOD'S REASON FOR SAVING US

What was God's reason for saving you? Was it just to get you to heaven? Was that the only reason He sent His Son? Absolutely not!

If getting you to heaven were God's only reason for saving you, then the moment you received Christ as your Lord and Savior, God would have killed you! That's right. Now that you are saved, His job would be complete. He might as well get you onward and upward to heaven. There would be no use for your hanging around here any longer!

But that wasn't the only reason He saved you. Instead of taking you immediately home, He placed a message in your heart—a message of good news about the eternal life that God has prepared for anyone who "will call upon the name of the Lord" (Rom. 10:13). Then He put you back on that scratch for a few more spins. But now there's a purpose to your life—a plan He has for you! Soon your life and mine will be over, but until He takes us home, we have a message to deliver.

Someone once said, "We will have all of eternity to boast about the victories won on the Earth, but we have only a few hours left in which to win them." When we get to heaven, we will see many wonderful things. But let me tell you of one thing we will never see again. We will never see another non-Christian. We will never have another opportunity for the rest of eternity to share the good news with someone who desperately needs the grace of God. The joy of heaven is when people come to a saving faith in Christ. These are the victories! What will we talk about for all of eternity if, when we arrive, we have not been about our Father's business? We must accomplish what God sent us onto this scratch to accomplish!

What will we talk about for all of eternity if we have not been about our Father's business?

HIS PLAN, OUR RESPONSIBILITY

A story is told of a Christian nurse who attended a very sick man confined to the intensive care unit of a hospital. Although the man was only in his early 60s, death seemed to loom closer with each passing day. The nurse would share the Lord with him and pray fervently for his salvation and healing. As the days slipped by, so did the man's chances for recovery. One evening, his breathing became so labored that the doctors feared he wouldn't make it through the night. His nurse spent extra hours that evening by his bedside praying for his healing.

The following morning, the nurse arrived back at work, expecting to find an empty bed. To her surprise, instead of an empty bed, she found her patient sitting up, eating breakfast and looking remarkably healthy!

"Praise the Lord!" she exclaimed. "You're healed!"

"Yup!" he cheerfully replied. "I feel great. You and your prayers . . . you healed me."

"Oh no! I didn't heal you," the nurse quickly replied. "God did. And now it is your responsibility to find out why."

God didn't save us so we could have access to someone who would answer all our prayers. God is not a genie in a lamp who is at our beck and call to answer our every whim. We are His servants. We belong to Him, and we exist for His purposes—not the other way around. He has saved us and given each of us a second chance. Now we must find out why. It's time we paused long enough to recalibrate our headings.

Jesus tells in Mark 8:36, "For what does it profit a man to gain the whole world, and forfeit his soul?" The application of this saying for someone who does not know Christ is obvious, but what is not so obvious is its application for us as Christians! For the follower of Christ, it could be applied in this way: What would it profit a Christian if all his prayers were answered— a fine house, abundant income, blessings galore—but he missed the very reason for which he was created? What a waste that would be!

Take a few moments and ask yourself why you think God created you. Why did He place you where you are? He makes no mistakes. You are on special assignment during your stay on Earth. As you read this book, let Him reveal to you what that is! He will if you ask Him. Watch, wait and see!

CHAPTER ONE STUDY GUIDE

1. Read John 15:16. God chose each of us for a reason. If God were to tell you six things that He wants your life to stand for, what would they be?

   a.

   b.

   c.

   d.

   e.

   f.

2. Why do you think God gave you certain gifts and placed you in a specific church?

3. What is one thing you want to accomplish before God takes you home? Write it below as a prayer.

CHAPTER TWO

DON'T FORGET
WHO YOU ARE

For our citizenship is in heaven.

PHILIPPIANS 3:20

THERE'S AN OLD STORY OF A RABBI LIVING IN A RUSSIAN CITY A CENTURY AGO. DISAPPOINTED BY HIS LACK OF DIRECTION AND LIFE PURPOSE, HE WANDERED OUT INTO THE CHILLY EVENING. WITH HIS HANDS THRUST DEEP INTO HIS POCKETS, HE AIMLESSLY WALKED THROUGH THE EMPTY STREETS, QUESTIONING HIS FAITH IN GOD, THE SCRIPTURES AND HIS CALLING TO MINISTRY. THE ONLY THING COLDER THAN THE RUSSIAN WINTER AIR WAS THE CHILL WITHIN HIS OWN SOUL. HE WAS SO ENSHROUDED BY HIS OWN DESPAIR THAT HE MISTAKENLY WANDERED INTO A RUSSIAN MILITARY COMPOUND THAT WAS OFF-LIMITS TO CIVILIANS.

The silence of the evening chill was shattered by the bark of a Russian soldier. "Who are you? And what are you doing here?"

"Excuse me?" replied the rabbi.

"I said, 'Who are you and what are you doing here?!'"

After a brief moment the rabbi, in a gracious tone so as not to provoke the soldier, said, "How much do you get paid every day?"

"What does that have to do with you?" the soldier retorted.

With some delight, as though he had just made a discovery, the rabbi said, "I will pay you the equal sum if you will ask me those same two questions every day: Who are you? and What are you doing here?"

Let me be that Russian soldier for you over these next few pages, as I ask you those same two questions:

"Who are you?" and "What are you doing here?"

JUST LIKE THE ISRAELITES

Beware lest you forget the LORD your God (Deut. 8:11).

Forgetfulness was a recurring problem for the children of Israel. We see in the Old Testament chronicles that forgetting who they were and thus forgetting the God they served was a common malady among the Israelites. The Lord often needed to remind them of who they were.

God had sternly warned the Israelites that if they should forget Him, the results could be disastrous:

> And it shall come about if you ever forget the LORD your God. . . . you shall surely perish. Like the nations that the LORD makes to perish before you (Deut. 8:19,20).

We often see in Scripture the Israelites building stone altars in the wilderness to signify a spot where God had done something spectacular, either a miracle of provision or one of victory. Ever wonder why? This was to remind them of who they were as a people and what they were supposed to be doing here. And when the children asked, "What are these stones?" the fathers would be able to tell them of God's greatness (see Josh. 4:20-24).

A SCARY THING TO FORGET WHO YOU ARE

A few summers ago, my son Aaron and three of his friends found a 55-gallon barrel and a sloping hill. The combination of these two discoveries by a group of teenage boys could only spell mischief. And so it did. They thought it would be great fun to get inside the barrel and roll one another down the hill.

The first to volunteer his life and future was Aaron. (I think he got his bravery from his mother.) The barrel took off from a slow, labored roll with Aaron inside, but it soon accelerated into an out-of-control, warp-speed, one-man suicide mission! The barrel began flipping end over end until it came to a crashing halt at the bottom of the hill. Somewhere along that wild ride, Aaron hit his head on the side of the flying barrel, and he was knocked out cold. When he finally regained consciousness a short time later, he couldn't remember a thing! He had sustained a concussion, and his memory was gone.

I was at a meeting when I received a call from one of his friends and partners in crime. He reported that Aaron had hit his head and had no recollection of anything that had taken place. I rushed home immediately to find a very frightened 16-year-old boy with temporary amnesia. Although Aaron is a virile, strapping young man, I had never seen him so afraid.

"Dad, I can't remember anything!" he said through the tears. "I'm so scared!" He wasn't entirely sure who he was. I tried reassuring him that his erased memory was only a temporary loss, that it would return in a day or so; and although the memory of the event itself may not, everything else should be fine. Despite my best efforts to assure him, Aaron remained scared and unsure.

Well, we drove him to the emergency room, and I had the dubious honor of explaining to the attending physicians how this concussion had come about. The doctors wheeled him into a room for a CAT scan, and about an hour later, the ER physician returned. He informed us that Aaron's memory would return in a day or two and that the scan of his brain came back normal, which frankly surprised me. After a stunt like that, I was shocked that they had found anything normal in there at all! I was thinking that it might be beneficial for each of his friends to take one of those scans, too.

Never forget why God called you and saved you!

We took Aaron home and, in fact, the following day his memory was back to normal, though he had no recollection of the traumatic event. Aaron eventually recuperated from his injury, and he came away with a little more wisdom about empty barrels, sloping hills and friends who are willing to nominate each another to boldly go where no one in his right mind has gone before. But I will always remember how scared my son was that day when he lost his memory of who he was.

When the people of Israel forgot who they were, there were no alarms, no sirens and no emergency 9-1-1 calls. With the occasional exception of a lone prophet, no one even noticed that anything might be wrong. Today we have a helper, the Holy Spirit, who reminds us that God has given us an identity and a purpose for living. Never forget why God called you and saved you!

EVERY MEMBER A MINISTER

In doing church as a team, this next principle is one of the most important. Ephesians 4:12 *(NKJV)* refers to "the equipping of the saints for the work of ministry." I always thought saints were those brave and wonderful Christians of years past who lived miraculously and died for their faith. But the Bible talks about *us* being saints, the people who are alive and doing "the work of ministry." You see, we are not only saints, but we are also to be ministers! In fact, Peter goes so far as to call us a "royal priest-hood" (1 Pet. 2:9)!

But somewhere along the line, we've forgotten who God created us to be. Instead of fulfilling our own calling, we hire others to do it for us. We interview a potential pastor, and if he can preach and do the business of the church, we hire him. Then after a few years, if he has done an adequate job of preaching, visiting the sick and performing weddings and funerals, we vote to "renew his call." He is the one who is supposed to do the ministry, so we just step out of his way.

As we have come to rely more and more heavily on the professional clergy, we have simultaneously developed a new breed of churchgoers: consumer Christians. A consumer Christian family can easily be spotted traveling from church to church, shopping for bargains and filling their empty basket of expectations with programs and personalities. After a reasonable period of searching, they settle on the church that most adequately fits the bill. They then begin to consume, and if at any time their rate of consumption is not equaled by the church's rate of feeding, they pack up and begin the search routine all over again.

Maybe it's time we return to the way God designed the Church to function in the first place. The ministry of the Church is not the responsibility of a few professionals; it is the divine responsibility of every single one of us.

Every member is a minister. That's what God says. In fact, He calls us to be full-time ministers! Full-time? Yes! Not just on Sundays, not just at Bible studies, but full-time.

Do we love God just part-time? Do we serve Him just part-time? We are all full-time citizens of heaven with a commission and an assignment to accomplish during our stay here on this planet.

Before you are a businessman, you are a minister. Before you are a homemaker, you are a minister. Before you are a student, a grandparent or a CEO, you are first a minister.

Some may protest, "But I don't work for the church! I work for the state (or the police department, a construction company, the department of education, a manufacturing firm). My company pays me, not my church! How can you say that I am a full-time minister?"

Sometimes we mistake the *channel* of our provision for the *source* of our provision. The Bible tells us that God is our provider, not a company or business. In fact, if you trace your paycheck back to its true source, it may take you to your place of employment, but it doesn't stop there! Like tracing a stereo wire, you'll find that if you keep following it, all our paychecks can be traced back to the very throne of God.

He is our provider. He chooses to use various places of employment through which He provides, but it is He who provides! Even if you're self-employed, the Bible reminds us, "But you shall remember (there's that word again!) the LORD your God, for it is He who is giving you power to make wealth" (Deut. 8:18).

WHAT'S THE BEST WAY TO REACH PEOPLE?

And he determined the times set for them and the exact places where they should live. God did this so that men would seek him and perhaps reach out for him and find him (Acts 17:26,27, *NIV*).

Have you ever asked yourself, *How does God plan to reach all the people living in my community?* Look again at Acts 17:26,27. God really has a plan, and yet so often we look at the overwhelming task of reaching our community and feel helpless. We simply shrug our shoulders and wonder to ourselves, *There are so many people scattered everywhere—and there's only one minister in our church to try and reach them all!*

Doing church as a team comes with a whole new way of looking at this dilemma.

Do you believe that God loves policemen? I do. Do you believe that He loves teachers? Me, too. What about construction workers? Absolutely! In fact, the Bible says, "The Lord is . . . not wishing for any to perish, but for *all* to come to repentance" (2 Pet. 3:9, emphasis added). And if He truly does love them and wants to reach them with the gospel, then what would be the very best way to do that?

Through a pastor? Possibly, but that may not be the most ideal. People at your office or school may be quite intimidated and even put off if a pastor walked into the lunchroom and began preaching.

What's the best way to reach teachers? It seems to me the best way would be through another teacher. So what does God do? He takes full-time ministers and disguises them as teachers! Yup! He takes saints like you and me, and He gives them gifts and a passion to be the best teachers they can be. Then He sends them into the school system where they can reach other educators with God's love.

How does God reach police officers? He takes full-time ministers and disguises them as police officers. He gives them the necessary gifts, passions and credentials, and He assigns them to police departments all over the nation.

How does He reach construction workers? He takes full-time ministers and disguises them as construction workers. He gives them the gifts and passions, makes them strong and hairy (excluding female workers, of course!), and He puts them to work at construction sites throughout every city.

God's full-time ministers are everywhere! We are all ambassadors. We are all ministers. Each one of us—not just pastors and evangelists—is called to represent Him in the world.

I have the privilege of pastoring a young, vibrant church in Hawaii, but my call to this church is no greater a call than that of anyone else! The pastor's role and responsibilities may differ somewhat from other roles, but the callings are the same: to be ministers for Christ.

So in every city, every town and every country, you will find full-time ministers, differently gifted and differently made, in every business and vocation. Like salt from a salt shaker, God takes us and scatters us everywhere to suit His flavor. He salts the Earth with His ministers, giving them gifts with which to influence their friends, families and coworkers and, as the old hymn goes, to reach "every kindred, every tribe on this terrestrial ball."[1]

You are the salt of the earth; but if the salt has become tasteless, how will it be made salty again? It is good for nothing anymore, except to be thrown out and trampled under foot (Matt. 5:13).

Don't lose your flavor, and don't forget who you are!

Note

1. "All Hail the Power of Jesus' Name" (1780), lyrics by Edward Perronet. The verse begins, "Let every kindred, every tribe, on this terrestrial ball, to Him all majesty ascribe, and crown Him Lord of all."

CHAPTER TWO STUDY GUIDE

1. Who are you? And what are you doing here? How would you answer these questions now?

2. The Israelites had a recurring problem of forgetting who God called them to be. Even after all the miracles and with all their feast days, still they would wander off. What might have caused this?

3. Do you agree that every member is a minister? What will it take for the people in our churches to catch this vision and rise to the challenge?

4. Whether you are a schoolteacher or a college student, whether among your family or friends, God can use you where you are! Each of us is designated to be a full-time minister. What are some of the ways God is calling you to minister within your unique sphere of influence?

5. Write down three names—one of a coworker or fellow student, an unsaved family member and an unsaved friend. Take a few minutes to pray for their salvation. Then ask God for an opportunity to share the gospel with them.

THE GIFTS: COMMISSIONED BEYOND OURSELVES

And since we have gifts that differ according to the grace given to us, let each exercise them accordingly.

ROMANS 12:6

GOD DOES SOMETHING VERY SPECIAL FOR EVERYONE ENTERING INTO HIS FAMILY. HE GIVES EACH NEW MEMBER A DIVINE ENDOWMENT KNOWN AS A SPIRITUAL GIFT (SEE 1 COR. 7:7; 1 PET. 4:10). THIS GIFT IS A GOD-GIVEN CAPACITY TO FULFILL WHAT HE HAS ASKED US TO ACCOMPLISH. THIS GIFT HELPS US TO LOCATE OUR NICHE, OUR PLACE AND OUR ROLE IN THE LIFE OF THE CHURCH. COMING TO GRIPS WITH THIS FACT MAY BE ONE OF THE MOST WONDERFUL DISCOVERIES OF YOUR LIFE!

Assigning someone to a task and equipping that person for the same are completely different issues. God knows that if we are to accomplish His will, we will not be able to do it in our own strength. We need something greater than ourselves. Even if we, in our own strength, happened to gain even a modicum of success, pride would swell us up like a puffer fish.

Gideon was like that, wasn't he? God asked him to fight against the massive forces of the Midianites, a marauding army of raiders. Prior to the battle, however, God deemed it necessary to prune Gideon's troops from 32,000 warriors to a measly 300! When Gideon asked God for the reason behind this seemingly suicidal decision, God answered, "The people who are with you are too many for Me to give Midian into their hands, lest Israel become boastful, saying, 'My own power has delivered me'" (Judg. 7:2).

God loves to take ordinary people like you and me and through them do extraordinary things! He doesn't need superheroes. He is looking for everyday believers, willing vessels whom He can equip and gift. Moreover, God not only gives us these divine endowments, but He also supplies the willingness to use them! Paul reminds us, "For it is God who is at work in you, both to *will* and to work for His good pleasure" (Phil. 2:13, emphasis added). When we function in the way God has gifted us to function, we can accomplish great things. And at the same time, we will find great joy in doing His will and His work!

GOD'S PROMISE CONCERNING HIS GIFTS

Now concerning spiritual gifts, brethren, I do not want you to be unaware (1 Cor. 12:1).

God has given each believer specific spiritual gifts to be discovered, developed and deployed—at least one. God doesn't want you to be unaware of yours. Why? Because knowing and functioning in your gift is at the very heart of the local church.

Remember the "Bo Knows" commercials by Nike in the 1980s? This award-winning series of ads poked fun at the notion that two-sports star Bo Jackson, who played both baseball and football professionally, could excel in any and every sport—Bo knows basketball, Bo knows auto racing, etc. In one commercial, an incredulous John McEnroe asks, "Bo knows *tennis?*" while hockey great Wayne Gretzky skates up to the camera, shakes his head and just says, "Uh-uh."

Doing church as a team doesn't mean one person doing a hundred things, superstar or not. That's how pastors burn out. Instead, this is about a hundred people doing one thing each—doing the one thing they have been gifted to do! This is not only possible—it is how God created us.

The question is not whether we have gifts. The real issue is whether we know what they are and are developing them for the Master's use:

> *As each one has received a special gift,* employ it in serving one another, as good stewards of the manifold grace of God (1 Pet. 4:10, emphasis added).

God has equipped us to serve through the use of our gifts, and if we are unaware of what they are, our ability to serve Him will be immensely impeded. God knew beforehand that His plan to reach the world could never be accomplished by an act of human will; it could only be accomplished through the strength He supplied in the form of spiritual gifts.

Let's take a closer look at how God equips His people. The Bible mentions three basic categories of gifts: office gifts, serving gifts and charismatic gifts.

THE OFFICE GIFTS

Therefore it says, "When He ascended on high, He led captive a host of captives, and *He gave gifts to men.*" And He gave some as apostles, and some as prophets, and some as evangelists, and some as pastors and teachers, for the *equipping* of the saints for the work of service, to the building up of the body of Christ (Eph. 4:8,11,12, emphasis added).

God established specific offices in the Church for the sake of oversight and leadership. Leadership is not exclusively reserved for these positions, but it is often carried out through them. However, what is of more interest to us in doing church as a team is the use of the word "equipping." The role of these offices is not to corner the market on ministry but, rather, to equip *God's people* to do the work of the ministry.

The Greek word translated as "equipping" in Ephesians 4:12 is very picturesque. It is the word *katartismos*, from the verb meaning "to mend." The word is earlier found in Mark 1:19, which shows the brothers James and John in a boat with their father, Zebedee, mending their nets. James and John were mending their nets, equipping themselves to catch more fish. The nets may have gotten snagged and torn on the rocky bottom of the Sea of Galilee, so they were being mended prior to the next fishing trip. The nets were being equipped for the purpose they were created for: to catch fish!

Pastors have the same role. They mend the saints, and they equip them. There will be many instances when hearing the Word of God will "mend" you, its truths impacting you in such a way that it brings wholeness and healing to a hurting area of your life or relationships. Through reading God's Word, you are increasingly equipped for the purposes to which God has called you. Its messages challenge you, reminding you of who you are and calling you forth to boldly use the gifts He's given you!

A fisherman does not mend his nets just to collect more mended nets! Neither is his goal to compete with other fishermen to see who can collect the biggest pile of nets. That would be ludicrous! He also doesn't mend nets to display them on his wall as trophies. So why does a fisherman mend his torn nets? To throw them back in the lake to catch more fish!

The same is true for each of us. God equips certain individuals with these office gifts in order to mend His people so that *we* will be equipped to do the work of the ministry. We are equipped so we—not just the evangelists—will "go into all the world and preach the gospel to all creation" (Mark 16:15). We are strengthened that we may discover and develop our gifts and then employ them "in serving one another" (1 Pet. 4:10). Paul says that as we do, the Body of Christ will be built up (see Eph. 4:12).

That's how churches grow! When the people are being consistently mended and equipped by the Word of God so that the work of the ministry is being done, churches become vibrant and healthy.

Under the traditional template of how church is done, the pastor does the work of the ministry and he gets as many people as he can to help him. In doing church as a team, the people do the work of the ministry—and they get the pastor to help them! That not only sounds better—it's biblical!

THE SERVING GIFTS

And since we have gifts that differ according to the grace given to us, let each exercise them accordingly: if prophecy, according to the proportion of his faith; if service, in his serving; or he who teaches, in his teaching; or he who exhorts, in his exhortation; he who gives, with liberality; he who leads, with diligence; he who shows mercy, with cheerfulness (Rom. 12:6-8).

Service gifts are distributed among Christians to equip us to excel in serving. Again, we must discover, develop and deploy these gifts if they are to be of any use. For example, if God says that your gift is teaching, then you must teach! If your gift is serving, then by all means, find a place and start serving! If your gift is leading, then for the sake of the kingdom of God, lead! To possess a gift and not use it is unthinkable and unacceptable to God.

Each of us must take the responsibility for the usage of our gifts. The assigned ministry of any church belongs to the people. As each of us discovers and begins to use our gifts, God is honored, the Body of Christ is built up, and we begin to know a sense of fulfillment greater than any we can find in the world.

The apostle Paul's lifelong goal was to discover the reason for his God-ordained birth:

Not that I have already obtained it, or have already become perfect, but I press on in order that I may lay hold of that for which also I was laid hold of by Christ Jesus (Phil. 3:12).

Paul pursued his gifting daily. His gift of apostleship was expressed in his passion to pioneer churches and to take the gospel to the Gentiles. God had chosen him for a specific purpose, gifted him for a specific reason, and Paul wasn't about to go home (to heaven) until he had fulfilled what God had laid hold of him for!

Serving in Your Passion

Allow me to take a slight detour for a moment and talk about a divine exclamation point that comes with using what God gives us. Along with special gifts, God gives to each of us certain passions—arenas of service that motivate us more than others. We've all seen musicians who have a passion for the piano above other musical instruments. Therefore, they play piano with a passion. We've all seen gifted athletes who are outstanding in one particular sport. They may possess the ability to excel in many different venues, but one sport catches their fancy more than the others do, and that is where they have poured all their time and energy. They excel in that sport and play it with passion!

Your passion is the area, or arena, where you feel most motivated to use your gift. Knowing your spiritual gift will answer the what question; knowing your passion will answer the where questions:

- Where shall I use my gifts?
- Where do I feel most motivated to serve?
- Where do I sense a calling or an attraction?

For some, their gift may be serving, while their *passion* is to help elderly people, so they minister to the needs of senior citizens. For others, their gift may be teaching, while their *passion* is discipleship, so they are drawn to small-group ministry. Others may find that their gift is music, while their passion is working with children, so they lead music in the children's ministry.

Link your gifts with your passion, and you will begin to play a powerful role in the Body of Christ. You will find such joy and motivation when this is taking place. When you are operating in your gift and passion, you will experience maximum effectiveness with a minimum of weariness. On the other hand, when you are *not* operating in your gift and passion, you will experience maximum weariness with a minimum of effectiveness. I'm sure every person reading this book has felt that kind of strain at one time or another!

*When operating in your gift and passion,
you will experience maximum effectiveness with
a minimum of weariness.*

THE CHARISMATIC GIFTS

Now there are varieties of gifts, but the same Spirit. For to one is given the word of wisdom through the Spirit, and to another the word of knowledge . . . to another faith by the same Spirit, and to another gifts of healing . . . to another the effecting of miracles, and to another prophecy, and to another the distinguishing of spirits, to another various kinds of tongues, and to another the interpretation of tongues. But one and the same Spirit works all these things, distributing to each one individually just as He wills (1 Cor. 12:4,8-11).

The charismatic gifts have long been the focus of tremendous controversy. The interpretation of this passage of Scripture has divided churches, segregated congregations and generally caused more havoc than whether or not a Christian should drink, dance, smoke, chew or hang around with girls who do.

God has authored every gift by His Spirit and placed them in the Church for the common good. Each congregation is designed to have a balance, with all the gifts represented and all the gifts functioning. Every gift—big or small, seen or unseen, on the platform or in the background—is crucial to a church's ability to operate with optimum effectiveness.

But what did we do? Somewhere along the way, we embraced all the gifts that looked like us and segregated the others. All those with certain gifts, such as tongues, miracles and prophecy, were grouped together under the label of "charismatic" or "Pentecostal." They so enjoyed each other's company that they began creating denominations based on the similarity of their gifts. Others gathered themselves according to the serving gifts (see Rom. 12:6-8) and became known as the "conservative" corner of the Church.

For years, these two factions would draw their lines, take their firing pins off safety, and never the twain would meet. The gifts became badges of honor, measurements of spirituality and terms of endearment.

Often, Christians will use similarity and familiarity as measuring rods for evaluating a church. If we enter a new church and they sing, talk, preach and act like us, that church passes the test;

and we will consent to have fellowship with them. On the other hand, if the congregation doesn't look like us or if they don't meet our expectations of what a church should be, then we conclude that this congregation is spiritually lacking; and they are deemed unworthy of our involvement.

But God never said, "Find a church where everyone in it looks like you." We are to find a church where everyone in it looks like *Him!*

Thank God, the kind of segregated thinking that has separated churches from one another is beginning to disappear. The Lord's original design was for all the gifts to function together, in harmony and with mutual respect. Every gift is necessary for what He desires to accomplish with His people. No one of us alone will possess all the gifts, but together we do! That's called the Church. There's nothing like the Church when it is vibrant, healthy and working like God designed it to work!

At New Hope Christian Fellowship, we welcome the totality of the gifts of the Holy Spirit as they were designed to function. We have many with the gift of serving, others with the gift of tongues, others with the gifts of leadership, teaching, mercy, giving and the rest. We all need each other!

When we need facilities set up or when we need to get a room ready for an activity, those with the gift of serving are always willing and ready. When a person needs prayer, we all pray, but there's nothing like someone with a gift of intercession who will pray with a passion until the request is answered—and it usually is! When the answer comes, all of us rejoice together.

When we need someone to oversee the hospital ministry, those with a mercy gift will usually be the first to step forward. When decisions are at an impasse, those with the gift of leadership are called upon, and they respond with great joy! The impasse is broken and the church moves forward again. When we need things organized, those who have the gift of organization get excited. They gladly step up, and they raise up phenomenal things from that which was once chaos.

If it weren't for each of us being willing and ready to use our individual gifts for the common good, our church would be in deep trouble! The more people serve one another through the willing use of their gifts, the more the respect factor for one another will rise until it goes through the roof.

We need each other.

NETA'S GIFT

Some time ago, I was to gather a few pastors for a morning meeting. I asked my secretary, Carol Ann, if she could put some pitchers of water on the tables and enough cups for the dozen pastors who were invited. Carol Ann is outstanding at recruiting people according to their gifts, so instead of doing something just to barely get by, she called Neta.

Now, Neta's gift is hospitality, so when Carol Ann asked if she wouldn't mind coming in and preparing the room, Neta was overjoyed! She went to work, picking fresh flowers and lining the tables with beautiful tablecloths. She filled water pitchers with ice-cold water, and she placed a scarf on each water jug, as if they were to be judged in competition for contemporary pitcher decor! Selected nuts in little bowls were neatly spaced on the tables, with candies and napkins adorning each place setting. The whole room took on a new appearance, and the aroma of fresh coffee, bagels and pastries filled the air. Neta had spent a full day preparing the room and making sure the ambiance was just right—and she loved doing it!

When I walked into the room the morning of the meeting, I thought I had stumbled into a photo shoot for *Better Homes and Gardens*. It was absolutely stunning! The visiting pastors felt so special that *I* would take the time to organize such a beautiful setting for their meeting. Well, all the credit went to Neta. Frankly if it were left to me, there would have been a few paper cups on each table so that they could retrieve their own water from the fountain downstairs.

After the meeting, Neta came up and asked, "Do you think you might be having any more of these soon? I just love doing these things!"

You see, Neta's gift is hospitality.

THE DANGER OF COMPARING GIFTS

One of the common pitfalls that hinders so many from finding their place in the Body of Christ is comparison. We start focusing on the kinds of gifts we don't possess rather than investing those that we do have. We try to look like, sound like and think like the people we admire most. In the end, this approach only leads to frustration with a half-baked, mediocre version of the gifting we were trying to imitate. The worst part of this is that our own creative energies start to dry up.

My wife, Anna, is from Springfield, Oregon. Some years ago, the Springfield Public Schools newsletter published a story that Chuck Swindoll alluded to in his wonderful book *Growing Strong in the Seasons of Life*. The story reminds us of how each of us is uniquely designed by the Master Architect.

Once upon a time, the animals decided they should do something meaningful to meet the problems of the new world. So they organized a school.

They adopted an activity curriculum of running, climbing, swimming and flying. To make it easier to administer, all the animals took all the subjects.

The duck was excellent in swimming. In fact, he was better than his instructor was! However, he made only passing grades in flying, and was very poor in running. Since he was so slow in running, he had to drop swimming and stay after school to practice running. This caused his webbed feet to be badly worn so he became only average in swimming. But "average" was quite acceptable, therefore nobody worried about it—except the duck.

The rabbit started at the top of his class in running, but developed a nervous twitch in his leg muscles because he had so much makeup work to do in swimming.

The squirrel was excellent in climbing, but he encountered constant frustration in flying class because his teacher made him start from the ground up instead of from the treetop down. He developed "charley horses" from overexertion, so he only got a "C" in climbing and a "D" in running.

The eagle was a problem child and was severely disciplined for being a non-conformist. In climbing classes, he beat all the others to the top, but insisted on using his own way of getting there![1]

The moral of this story is that each of us has been given his or her own gifts, capabilities and passions, and we will be inclined to excel in certain activities. If we concentrate on pointing out each other's weaknesses, however, we may seem spiritual or vigilant, but we won't be fruitful or very helpful.

You see, everybody is a 10 . . . somewhere. When we compare ourselves with one another, we can also become blinded to the wonderful qualities God has woven into our own design. A better way would be for each of God's creatures to develop his or her own gifts, while at the same time learning to respect the gifts of others.

God isn't into making clones. We are not all the same; He never intended for us to be. God placed each of us in His family with a certain mixture of gifts, temperaments and capabilities. When we operate within our individual roles and realms of gifting, we will be much more likely to excel. Not only will we tremendously benefit the Body of Christ, but we will also experience incredible joy!

In order to accomplish what God has intended for us as individuals and as a whole, we must do church as a team. A 99 percent involvement is still 1 percent shy! We need all of us functioning in our gifts, with respect and love for each other. That's what the local church body is all about. No one is unimportant. Everyone is a part of sharing the gospel, not just the pastor. We do church as a team!

Booker T. Washington, the most influential black leader and educator of his time in America, once said, "No race can prosper till it learns that there is as much dignity in tilling a field as in writing a poem."[2] If I understand correctly what he said, it is this: Every single person is incredibly important to the fulfillment of God's plan. Take hold of that! *No one is unimportant.* Let that truth burn within your soul. The ministry belongs to you and me, and it requires both of us to be involved. Doing church is not the responsibility of the professional clergy and a few talented staff people.

The strength of a church is not found in the beauty of its building, the number of attendees or the size of the budget. Remember, a church is only as strong as its members, and the more each person takes ownership in the ministry of the church, the stronger it becomes. Only when we realize that God has called every single one of us with an equally divine imperative can the Church and its congregations begin to reach their fullest potential.

So relax! Enjoy who God created you to be. Rest in Him and cultivate your gifts and God-given capabilities. Don't compare yourself with others, and don't be worried about what you don't have. Instead, put to use what you *do* have! Don't bemoan your weaknesses. Strengthen your strengths!

There's plenty of room for every creature, every gift and every style.

WATCHING IT ALL COME TOGETHER

I think the first time I really saw it all come together was at one of our Christmas Eve services in 1996. We had a program filled with multimedia presentations, dance, mime, drama, a 100-voice choir and ensembles—I mean, the works! The auditorium was filled with more than 1,200 people, many who were there for the very first time. I stood just offstage, watching the evening unfold.

During the past year, our first in Oahu, we had seen more than 1,400 people open their hearts to Christ. Whenever you gather so many new believers in one place, you will have fire! The evening's music erupted with a song of magnificent celebration. Dancers burst onto the stage, expressing the exuberance of the song with cartwheels and twists. A former university cheerleader came bounding across the platform with flips and somersaults. Others were tossed into the air for the finale, and the auditorium broke into applause. (They threw a couple of the girls so high, we haven't heard from them since!)

Sometime during this program, it hit me. As I watched our outstanding keyboardist, Steve Kenny, play the piano with all his heart, I thought to myself, *Steve is preaching the gospel the best way he knows how—through his piano!*

Nearby, Clarke Bright was playing the drums with his usual excellence. People sometimes say they like to watch Clarke play because he plays more with his heart than he does with his drumsticks. That night I said to myself, *Clarke is preaching the gospel the best way he knows how—through his drums!*

I looked into the radiant faces of the choir, where I saw many lives that had recently been transformed by the Lord's grace, and I said to myself, *Those wonderful people are all preaching the gospel the best way* they *know how—through their singing!* The mime, the drama team and the ensemble were all preaching the gospel through their gifts.

Then I noticed the stage coordinators moving with poise and rhythm, rearranging microphones and straightening cords. I saw our video people running the cameras. I looked out over the audience and observed the ushers greeting people with genuine enthusiasm. I spotted the faces of different individuals who had brought along friends and neighbors. All these people were preaching the gospel through their gifts, passions and talents.

At the end of a memorable program, I walked out onto the platform, picked up a microphone and wrapped up the evening with a simple presentation of the gospel message. Yes, through speaking I too was preaching the gospel the best way I knew how, but I wasn't doing it alone. We were all doing it together! We were preaching the gospel the best way we knew how—through our gifts. And that included the children's workers, parking team and everyone who had worked behind the scenes to make this evening happen. Every single person had a part.

This event was not one presentation of the gospel but several hundred presentations of the gospel—all at the same time in one evening. That's what made it so powerful!

I started to see it clearly, and I was flooded with a whole new understanding of how beautiful the Body of Christ can be.

We were doing church as a team!

Notes

1. Chuck Swindoll, *Growing Strong in the Seasons of Life* (Sisters, OR: Multnomah Publishers, 1984), p. 312.
2. Booker T. Washington, *Up from Slavery* (1901), quoted in John Bartlett, *Familiar Quotations*, 15th edition, p. 681.

CHAPTER THREE STUDY GUIDE

1. Each Christian has at least one spiritual gift. Look up the
   following Scripture verses. What does each one tell us about
   the gifts?

   a. 1 Corinthians 12:1

   b. Romans 12:6-8

   c. 1 Corinthians 12:4,8-11

   d. Ephesians 4:8-12

2. Why do you think the issue of spiritual gifts has divided the
   Church?

3. What is your understanding of how the gifts should operate
   together in any one church? Should the gifts be segregated?
   Why or why not?

4. What are your spiritual gifts? How do you know? List them below.

5. With your gifts in mind, in what possible ministries would you fit well?

6. If you could do any ministry at all in the local church that would make every day seem like Christmas for you, which ministry would you choose?

CHAPTER FOUR

FINDING YOUR FIT

For it is God who works in you to will and to act
according to His good purpose.

PHILIPPIANS 2:13, *NIV*

EACH OF US IS LIKE A PIECE OF A JIGSAW PUZZLE. EVERY PIECE HAS ITS PLACE IN GOD'S PLAN. NO ONE PIECE IS OPTIONAL. HOW FRUSTRATING IT WOULD BE TO PUT TOGETHER A 3,000-PIECE PUZZLE ONLY TO FIND ONE OF THE PIECES MISSING AT THE END! THAT'S HOW GOD SEES US. EVERY PIECE IS INCREDIBLY IMPORTANT! EVERYONE IS NECESSARY TO COMPLETE THE DIVINE PUZZLE. WHEN ALL THE PIECES FIT TOGETHER, THE WORLD CAN SEE A BEAUTIFUL, COMPLETED PICTURE OF THE HEART OF JESUS FOR PEOPLE EVERYWHERE.

How do we find our place in God's plan? Will it come easily? Where do we start? As with any puzzle, each piece doesn't smoothly fall into place on the first attempt. It usually takes several tries in order to find the right fit. You turn the piece this way and that, set it aside and try a few others, and then you try it again. If a piece doesn't fit on the first go-round, you don't toss the rebellious piece into the trash! No, you keep at it because you know every piece is a perfect fit . . . somewhere.

But I am just one piece, you might rationalize. *They can do without me. Why, there are 2,999 other pieces! I'm just one, insignificant piece. They'll never miss me.*

Don't you dare think that way! That's exactly how the enemy of our souls wants you to think of yourself, but don't you do it—even for a minute. You are vital to the success of our mission!

BREAKING THROUGH OUR LIMITATIONS

Each of us knows what it means to be sentenced to limitations placed on our lives by ourselves and others. The artificial, perceived limitations could be the result of our upbringing, past circumstances, a parent's comments, past failures and even the judgment of our friends. These mental ceilings restrain us from discovering our fullest potential.

But God's power is available to each and every one of us. He is able even when we are not. He is strong when we are weak and, regardless of how we feel, God always provides a way! If we are going to become what God has designed us to be, we must discover these false ceilings in our lives and break through them.

Have you ever been to a circus and seen elephants perform? Their strength is incredible. When I was ten years old, I spotted one of these mighty creatures outside the big top, and in my innocent way, I crawled under the rope to get a closer look. I was shocked to see that this huge elephant was restrained only by a tiny rope attached to a foot-long stake in the dirt! The monstrous pachyderm would wander the full length of the rope and, when it felt a little tug, it would stop. With one flick of its huge foot, that elephant could have sent that stake flying through the air (and flattened me) with the greatest of ease!

Later, I asked one of the caretakers about this. He explained that when an elephant is very young, its owners tie it to a very strong stake. After pulling and tugging on the restraint to no avail, the elephant eventually figures that further attempts to get loose are hopeless. So the elephant no longer tries. When the elephant is fully grown, it still has this limitation in its mind. (Remember, an elephant never forgets!) Now all the caretaker has to do is to put a little stake in the ground, attach a flimsy rope to its foot, and the elephant won't go anywhere. Why? Because it doesn't believe that it can! The huge animal has been conditioned to think small.

How much potential do you have? How willing are you to reach for God's fullest measure? Let's take a look at your potential for a moment.

Your potential is like an iceberg that is 10 percent above the water with the other 90 percent hidden beneath the surface. Your potential is represented by the whole iceberg, but most of us use only the 10 percent above the water. With God's help, you can put your whole potential to its fullest use for the Lord!

Use the following blanks to rate yourself on how much of your potential you are currently reaching. Write a percentage in the space next to each category. How do you fare?

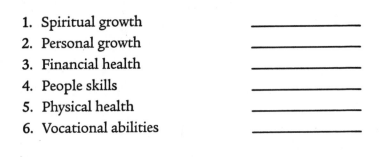

1. Spiritual growth   _____
2. Personal growth   _____
3. Financial health   _____
4. People skills   _____
5. Physical health   _____
6. Vocational abilities   _____

7. Family health   _____
8. As a leader in church   _____
9. Relationship with friends   _____

FINDING YOUR DESIGN

God doesn't want you to settle for anything less than His very best. You have been created with special talents, abilities and gifts. That's wonderful in itself, but what's even more important is how you invest those qualities. You must discover and develop your talents, abilities and gifts to their fullest potential; only then will you be able to crash through your barriers of limitation.

There are many wonderful courses you can take that will help you find your gifts and passions. One of the ways we at New Hope determine our gift mix is through the DESIGN course. This course is taught twice each year at our Doing Church as a Team conferences. There is no guarantee that a person's full mixture of gifts will be accurately pinpointed by graduation, but I do guarantee that each participant will come away with a much greater appreciation and understanding of his or her gifts. The more you understand the way the Lord designed you to be, the better you will be able to cooperate with His design.

DESIGN is an acrostic that stands for the different ingredients that, when combined, equal *you*. When you recognize and develop each of these six categories, you'll be on your way to realizing your full potential in Christ!

D for Desire

What is your passion? If all things were equal and you could do anything in the world for the Lord, what job would you choose to do—something that would make every day feel like Christmas? God has placed certain desires in you as one way of telling you what He wants you to do. He has not only given you certain abilities, but He has also given you the desire to pursue exactly what He's asked you to do! Philippians 2:13 tells us, "It is God who is at work in you, both to *will* and to *work for* His good pleasure" (emphasis added). That's incredible!

E for Experience

Your past experiences are important considerations when seeking and finding your design. What tasks or projects have influenced you in the past? God will use even negative experiences to complete your design. What have you learned from the times when you have been hurt? How have they made you more compassionate toward others in similar situations?

God will never waste a hurt. One of my favorite Bible verses is Psalm 56:8, which says, "Thou hast taken account of my wanderings; put my tears in Thy bottle; are they not in Thy book?"

God has put all your tears in a bottle. In other words, He remembers them all and will use them for your good. Some people think that because of their past or the way they were raised, they will find it impossible to succeed in this world. Consider a few examples of people who overcame past obstacles. You may recognize some of these names.

He didn't talk till he was four years old, and he didn't start to read till he was seven. One of his teachers labeled him as "mentally slow, unsociable and adrift in his foolish dreams." This was often said of young *Albert Einstein*.

"He's too stupid to learn anything," said some of the teachers of a young boy named *Thomas Edison*.

"He possesses minimal football knowledge and lacks motivation," an expert said of a beginning coach named *Vince Lombardi*.

He went bankrupt several times and was fired by the editor of a local newspaper because he apparently had a lack of ideas. The man they fired was *Walt Disney*.

He failed the sixth grade and experienced a lifetime of setbacks and defeats. Finally, as a senior citizen, *Winston Churchill* became the prime minister of England.

S for Spiritual Gift

Every person who knows Jesus Christ is endowed with one or more spiritual gifts. These are enumerated in 1 Corinthians 12, Romans 12, Ephesians 4 and 1 Peter 4. God never intended for Christ's ministry to cease when He ascended into heaven, so He decided that His ministry would be carried on through those who believed. Knowing that we could never do it on our own, God sent His Spirit, who distributed gifts to the Church through which we would carry on His work. What are your spiritual gifts? Are you willing for God to use you in any of them?

I for Individual Style

Each of us has a unique temperament that we call a personality, or individual style. Some of us are more extroverted, while others tend toward being more introverted. We all know "people persons" and others who are more task oriented. Some live very structured lives, while others are impetuously spontaneous.

Your individual style will not change your calling as a Christian, but it will tell you how to carry out your calling. Each of us must run the race set before us. We may each do it differently, but the main thing is that we run the race!

I have never been a salesman. I remember a time when I was supposed to sell tickets for a school project. I begged my dad to buy them all, so I wouldn't have to sell them door-to-door. Another time I took all the money I had saved to pay for a case of almond chocolates our school was selling—25 bars at a dollar per bar! Later, I gave them away as gifts.

When I became a Christian in college, I attended a course in evangelism held by Campus Crusade for Christ, an outstanding group founded by Bill Bright. They perfected and published *The Four Spiritual Laws*, a little booklet used to win many to Christ. An entire morning class was devoted to how to use this booklet. Then came the moment of truth. Our final project was that we were to go door-to-door and share the Four Spiritual Laws with our neighbors for the last two hours. I wanted to die! All the other students seemed so excited, and I felt like such a worm because I didn't want to win anyone to the Lord.

While everyone else was zealously banging on doors, I quietly found a McDonald's nearby, read my Bible for two hours and repented that I couldn't bring myself to lead anyone to the Lord. When everyone returned with glowing reports, I just sat there in the corner of the room hoping no one would notice me. I felt guilty and condemned, unworthy to be called a Christian.

On the other hand, I love the arts. I love music, creative multimedia presentations, storytelling and songwriting. Over the years, I've pursued these with a passion. In Bible college, I formed a musical group that traveled throughout the country each summer, singing and speaking at dozens of youth camps. Through the use of the arts and through public speaking, I have seen hundreds of people come to Christ. During the first year of New Hope in Oahu, God allowed me to be a small part of more than 1,800 people receiving Christ for the first time! I was humbled to learn this. That is equivalent to five people a day being won to Christ!

My calling is still the same, although my design will dictate the style that I am most comfortable with.

G for Growth Phase

Each of us is still growing in the Lord. Some of us may be spiritual toddlers, while others are more like adolescents or adults. Some have knowledge but have a long way to go in gaining wisdom—that is, the ability to apply that knowledge to everyday living. Others are fountains of common sense but know very little of the Bible.

There's a common misconception that spiritual growth can be measured by the time one has spent in the Church. The truth of the matter is that in one or two years, a person who is intent on following the Lord can be much more mature and laden with insight and wisdom than another Christian who, even after a dozen years, simply cruises along without much involvement.

We have to remember that Jesus turned over the responsibility for administrating the whole Church to a few former fishermen and tax gatherers who were just three years old in the Lord! Christian growth is measured more by a person's willingness to apply what he has heard than it is by his length of stay in the pews. John 13:17 reminds us, "If you know these things, you are blessed if you *do* them" (emphasis added).

Are you an infant, toddler, adolescent, young adult or a mature adult in your relationship with Christ? Your current growth phase is factored as part of your DESIGN.

N for Natural Abilities

All of us have seen natural athletes who seem able to excel in any sport they take up. Other people have natural abilities in other areas, such as computers, working with children, mechanics, electronics or problem solving. Our natural abilities are an important component of who God made us to be.

What do you enjoy doing? Do you have a natural talent for fixing things? What about strategic planning, financial planning, working with the elderly or working with babies? When we work within our design, life gets exciting and fun. You see, God isn't some unbending drillmaster who demands your service. He really wants your heart! He tells us in Deuteronomy 28:47,48, "Because you did not serve the LORD your God with joy and a glad heart, for the abundance of all things; therefore you shall serve your enemies." You see, God doesn't just want us to serve Him; He wants us to serve Him joyfully! Then we will be functioning in the way God designed us to function.

Add all these components together, and you'll find your DESIGN. These ingredients will help you to find the shape and placement of your puzzle piece. Now all you need to add to this recipe is involvement!

PATIENCE: THE BREAKFAST OF CHAMPIONS

Finding your fit may take time. Be patient. God may want to build quality of character before He fits you into your niche. In any case, be patient. Everything has an order to it, and we can't push our way into God's plan.

When most people start on a puzzle, the first thing they usually do is to fit the edge pieces together, forming a sort of frame. The outer edge is the easiest part of the puzzle to assemble because each of the border pieces has at least one side with a straight edge. Then you start working your way toward the middle.

Finding your fit in a church is not unlike this process. Like fitting the pieces of a puzzle together, it requires patience! Sometimes you'll see others getting assigned to tasks almost immediately. When that happens, there will be a tendency to label these people as part of the in crowd, while you struggle with feeling like an outsider.

Relax! Like the inner pieces of a puzzle, you'll need to be patient. You may not be able to find your fit until two or three other edge pieces find theirs first. Then, lo and behold, you might very well be that piece which joins them all together!

So don't give up, even if you think that you're just one measly, unimportant piece. You'd be surprised at the power of just one. You can make a huge difference!

In 1645, one vote gave Oliver Cromwell control of England.

In 1776, one vote made English the official language of the United States instead of German, at least according to folklore.

In 1845, one vote brought Texas into the Union. Later, California, Oregon, Washington and Idaho were admitted to the Union, and the purchase of Alaska was ratified—all by a single vote.

In 1868, one vote saved President Andrew Johnson from being impeached.

In 1876, one vote gave Rutherford B. Hayes the U. S. presidency.

In 1923, one vote gave Adolph Hitler control of the Nazi Party.[1] You are just one, but you count!

THREE RESULTS OF USING YOUR GIFTS

God designed each of us to be intricately involved in His plan. When you are willing to launch out and use your gifts for the sake of the Kingdom, three wonderful things will begin to happen: You will know amazing joy, enjoy healthy accountability and experience accelerated spiritual growth.

When you launch out and use your gifts for the sake of the Kingdom, wonderful things will begin to happen.

Amazing Joy

You will experience amazing joy when you are operating in your gift. The Greek word for spiritual gifts is *charismata*, which is derived from the word *charis*, or grace. The root word of grace? It is the word *chara*, which means joy! Yes, joy is at the very root of the use of your spiritual gift.

In his book *Anatomy of an Illness*, Norman Cousins tells a story of the latter years of Pablo Casals, one of the great musicians of the twentieth century. On the morning of his 90th birthday, Casals's arthritis and frailty were so debilitating that it was almost unbearable to watch him begin his day. His emphysema was evident in his labored breathing. Casals walked with a shuffle, stooped over with his head pitched forward. His hands were swollen, his fingers clenched, and he looked every inch a very tired old man.

But that day, even before eating breakfast, Pablo Casals made his way to the piano, one of the instruments on which he had become very proficient. Laboriously and with great difficulty, he arranged himself on the piano bench. It seemed like such a terrible effort for him to bring his clenched, swollen fingers to the keyboard.

Then something miraculous happened. Casals began to be completely transformed. As he played this instrument he so loved, moving where he was so gifted, his physiology changed and produced in his body (and on the piano) a result that should have only come from a strong, healthy individual. His fingers slowly unclenched and reached for the keys like the tendrils of a plant reach toward the sunlight. Casals began with a rendition of Bach, then moved on to a Brahms concerto, racing his fingers across the keyboard. His whole body seemed to be fused with the music. His frame was no longer stiff and shrunken but graceful and completely freed from the arthritic bondage.

By the time he walked away from the piano, Casals seemed an entirely different person. He stood taller and walked without a trace of a shuffle. He immediately moved to the breakfast table, ate a hearty meal and then went out for a stroll along the beach! [2]

What a wonderful story of belief and renewal! It graphically illustrates how God has designed us to function in our gifts. When we do, we live vibrantly!

A Healthy Accountability

If you are a solo artist, you don't need accountability. You don't need to keep rhythm with anyone else. You're it—the big cheese! But when you're using your gifts and doing church as a team, you need to match your stroke to the other members of the team. You need to show up when you are scheduled to. You need to hang in there when the going gets tough. You can't just quit when the winds pick up. You are required to be accountable!

Why is accountability so important? Without accountability, we will never build character. Watch those who have chosen to dodge accountability. They look good in the calm; but when the storm hits, they usually are no match for the stresses and currents, and it isn't long before they capsize. Character is the inner strength that carries you to the finish. Character is the weight in our lives, and accountability is our weight trainer. Accountability is one of God's favorite tools for building the character we need.

Michael Plant was one of the world's best yachtsmen. Numerous times he navigated the Pacific Ocean as well as the Atlantic as a solo voyager. Through those experiences Plant gained skill and notoriety. In 1992, he decided to go all the way.

He purchased a state-of-the-art sailboat with the best navigational equipment money could buy. His dreamboat was christened *The Coyote*. On this boat was an emergency global positioning locator. With one press of a button, the system would transmit a signal that would be picked up by satellite. Within a few seconds, either of two ground locations could pinpoint Plant's coordinates, even in the middle of the vast ocean. *The Coyote* was the most fail-safe vessel of its kind.

Early in the fall of 1992, Plant set out from the East Coast on a solo voyage, destination France. On the fourth day of the voyage, ground locators lost contact with *The Coyote*. Weather scans of the Atlantic showed storms causing high seas, and it was assumed that Plant was navigating the storms and would soon regain contact. But he never did.

Search-and-rescue squads were deployed to the last known location of *The Coyote* but to no avail. Commercial airliners were asked to monitor their emergency channels in case Plant was broadcasting signals for help.

Two weeks after his departure, a ship about 400 miles off the Azores came upon *The Coyote* floating upside down. If there's one position where a state-of-the-art global positioning locator will not be of much use, it's upside down.

Hoisting *The Coyote* up for a closer look, the rescuers searched the cabin, hoping to find the emergency life raft already deployed, which would indicate that Michael Plant might still be alive and floating somewhere in the Atlantic. But they found the life raft only partially inflated, still stuck in the hull of the boat. To this day, the body of Michael Plant has never been found.

The telltale culprit in the accident was a broken keel. No one knows whether *The Coyote* hit some ocean sewage, a submarine or a whale, but the ballast had been broken off, leaving the boat without any weight in the keel. The ballast was an 8,000-pound weight placed in the keel, making this sailboat one of the safest vessels on the ocean. Because of the amount of weight in the keel, even should it capsize, the design of the ballast would roll it upright again. Yet without the weight in the keel, *The Coyote* was no match for the storms of the Atlantic.

I don't know much about sailing, but one thing I do know: To have stability in a storm, there must be *more weight beneath the waterline than above it*. Without ballast, a boat can look fine in the bay or in calm water. Its sails may be unfurled and its colors flying, but without any weight in its keel, the boat is unable to launch any further into the deep. One person said it this way: "Ships are safe in the harbor, but that's not what ships were made for."

Character is the weight beneath our waterline. Without it, we may look good in the harbor. We can fly our colors and strut our stuff, but we will be no match for the currents. Storms alone don't develop character. They may reveal character, but only genuine accountability will build it.

Accelerated Growth

God designed us to make use of our gifts. We were created to serve, anointed to serve and gifted to serve. That's God's plan. In fact, using our gifts to serve is a crucial and indispensable ingredient for spiritual growth. It's all part of the package.

Last year, we took a tour to Israel. One of my favorite stops was the Dead Sea. It's a beautiful, expansive lake touching Jordan's borders on its eastern shore and Israel in the west. The mineral deposits of the Dead Sea are abundant, making it one of the richest spots on the face of the earth. Normal seawater contains about 4 percent mineral content, giving it a salty taste. The Dead Sea has a mineral content of 22 percent! Scattered throughout the lake you can see pillars of salt reaching toward the surface like lone soldiers waiting for a command. The water, which resembles baby oil more than it does ocean water, lazily laps the shores.

As beautiful and rich as the Dead Sea is, however, you won't see any of the familiar sites usually seen around Middle Eastern lakes. There are no fishing villages, no boats, no drying nets, no villagers haggling over fish prices or sea gulls gliding overhead. Why? Because nothing lives in the Dead Sea—hence, its name. The heavy mineral content makes the water uninhabitable for fish or any of the other living creatures common to nearby lakes, such as the Sea of Galilee. The Dead Sea is rich but dead—abundant and wealthy but lifeless.

The main reason for the absence of life is that there is no outlet. For eons, the headwaters of the Jordan have fed this lake, freely depositing her mineral treasures found along the way. But because the Dead Sea is a cul-de-sac in a desert that's nearly 1,200 feet below sea level, its intake of water is released only through evaporation. There is no other outlet. There are no currents of water, no flowing tributaries and no life to embrace within its shores.

Churches can turn into dead seas, rich in content but lifeless. There is only one way to begin the life process flowing, and that's to open up an outlet! We've got to get our gifts moving and our hearts serving, and then the currents of life will reappear. Every congregation runs the risk of entropy and stagnation. A church can look good from afar but, like the fig tree, may be scarce in fruit up close. Using our gifts to do church as a team is a nonnegotiable part of growth.

People are like sponges. If a sponge is put under a faucet of running water, it soon becomes saturated. Once that happens, you can run the water over it all day, but it won't be able to absorb any more water. The only way to restore the sponge's absorbency is to wring it out!

As Christians, we absorb teaching, instruction, God's Word and His promises; but at some point along the way, we stop growing. We get saturated and our capacity to absorb is diminished. No matter how many more messages we hear, we are unable to absorb any more until we wring out our sponges. Then, and only then, will our absorbency return.

Wring out your sponge and serve! Don't hang on to the water. Give it freely away. There's plenty more where that came from!

When I was in high school, I was a novice guitar player. I would add about one new chord a month to my repertoire of musical knowledge. This was a slow boat to guitar proficiency, but I figured that slow and steady was better than not having launched at all. I would dream about being in a band, playing guitar for school dances and proms, but at my present pace, I calculated that it would take me another 170 years before I'd be ready to perform in public.

Nevertheless, my big chance came at the end of my junior year. Just before summer break began, the lead guitarist of the top band in our school approached me. They were looking for a rhythm guitarist and lead vocalist. He asked if I would consider joining up with them. I was flabbergasted! This was my dream come true. Of course I said yes!

Only one catch: The summer schedule of the band started in three weeks, and I had to learn 20 new songs. We would hold practice three times a week until we got the new songs down.

I was so excited, I couldn't sleep at night! I sang those songs over and over until I memorized every word, every move and every chord. Each waking moment was dedicated to learning. I can't even remember whether or not I passed my finals that year. (I suppose I did.) One thing I do remember is that before I joined a band, my growth rate on the guitar was minimal at best. But as soon as I got involved, my growth accelerated at least 200 percent! I learned chords I didn't even know existed! I had boundless energy and looked forward to playing guitar at every opportunity.

Getting involved in your church by using your gifts will accelerate your spiritual growth immensely. God designed us that way.

Don't head for the grandstands when you enter the kingdom of God. Head for the playing field. That's where the excitement is. That's where the action is.

But most importantly, that's where our Coach is!

THE FASTEST WAY TO THE THRONE

> But when you are invited, go and recline at the last place, so that when the one who has invited you comes, he may say to you, "Friend, move up higher"; then you will have honor in the sight of all who are at the table with you. For everyone who exalts himself shall be humbled, and he who humbles himself shall be exalted (Luke 14:10,11).

Let us consider the heart of a servant. Regardless of a person's gifts, talents or abilities, each of us is called to the foot of the table. That's more a matter of the heart than it is a matter of giftedness. One of our favorite sayings at New Hope is "The fastest way to the throne will always be through the servant's entrance." Jesus modeled servanthood to us, and when we develop our gifts, we begin by coming through the servant's entrance. This is the heart behind serving. Whatever the need is, we need to be willing to pick up a towel and wash someone's feet.

Using your gifts in a church is not always a guarantee that God will bless you. Your gifts must be used with the right heart and with right motives. Sometimes people use gifts to justify their behavior. If there's a distasteful job to be done, a person may say, "Oh, that just isn't my gift. That's not my passion." When that happens, it is usually not an issue of gifts or passions; rather, it is an issue of the heart.

There is a tendency in each of us to use religious cloaks to justify selfish motives. It's nothing new. All our lives, the arrows of attention and interest have been turned inward, and some of those arrows are difficult to redirect. Turning them away from ourselves takes daily effort and a constant commitment to purity and the development of a servant heart.

The late Mother Teresa has spoken to my heart through her books over the years. She was an incredible leader who exemplified for me the untiring heart of a servant. In the classic book *The Love of Christ*, Mother Teresa speaks of her magnificent work in Calcutta. She reflects:

> What we are doing is but a drop in the ocean. This may be only a drop, but the ocean would be less if it weren't there. What we do is something small, but we do it with big hearts. At death, we will not be judged by the amount of work we did, but by the amount of love we put into it. We do not strive for spectacular actions. What counts is the gift of yourself, the degree of love you put into each of your deeds. . . . Do you want to be great? Pick up a broom and sweep the floor.[3]

I love that. Here was a servant whom God used to touch a needy world. She was content to serve an "Audience of One," as Greg Ferguson so aptly composed. She didn't clean tables with a washcloth; she cleaned them with her heart. She didn't give speeches with eloquence; she gave them with her heart.

When you serve, serve with your heart. Whether you teach, sing, pass out bulletins, play an instrument, set up chairs or clean tables, always remember: It's not the size of the task but the size of the heart you put into the task that makes what you do something beautiful for God!

DESERVING OF OUR BEST

One of New Hope's core values is that God is worthy of our very best. We have coined a saying around the church: "Simplicity with Excellence." Because everything we do is for an audience of One, everything matters! Whether we're cleaning a table or rolling up a microphone cord, God does not deserve our left-overs. He deserves the best we can give!

Excellence is very different from perfection or opulence, which are not what the Lord expects of us. A spirit of excellence, a quality found in the life of Daniel (see Dan. 1:17-20; 5:12; 6:3), is a constant desire to give our first fruits—our very best in all we do because we are serving the King of kings.

Some months ago, a clothing store called me and asked if I would come and pick up a few boxes. They wanted to donate them to a worthy cause. They said that one of the bosses from the corporate headquarters was coming in; they needed to spruce up the place, and the boxes were in the way. Our director of Care Ministries, Mark Hovland, and I had just been talking about set-ting up a thrift store in our church, so the invitation to pick up some items from a clothing outlet really excited me. Maybe they would have enough clothing to get the thrift store started!

When I arrived at the store, the manager gave me two large boxes to load into my car. I didn't even ask about the contents. Grateful for the donation, I simply thanked him and left.

As soon as I arrived home, I opened the boxes to see what might be the beginnings of our new ministry. To my surprise and disappointment, the boxes contained nothing I had expected or hoped for. They were filled with broken, soiled and returned items that the store deemed beyond repair: broken purses, mis-matched earrings, torn clothing, pants with broken zippers and scratched sunglasses. My heart sank! Every item had been returned to the store because of some defect. The store had thrown these items into boxes, and the management needed to dispose of them. They had decided these items would go either to the dump or to the church. This time, I guess, the church won.

I did what I could to repair the items that were salvageable and disposed of the rest. I was amused when, two days later, the manager called and asked me for a tax-deductible receipt!

After musing over these things, I came to a gripping thought. *Where did they learn this? Who taught them that if they had a choice between trashing something or giving it to God, that it would be a nice, benevolent thing to at least let God have it?*

We have taught them those lessons!

Over the years, we as Christians have modeled this behavior quite well. We clean out our closets once a year; and if we find old sweaters with holes in them, pants that don't fit or things we can't use anymore, we give those things to the church!

God deserves the very first of our hearts, not our last. When you worship, worship with everything that is within you! If you serve, serve Him with all you've got! If you sing, sing your heart out! Train, don't just try. Prepare, don't just perform. Practice, don't just pray. Do both, and in doing so, you will be giving God your best. Everything matters because He deserves our everything!

Notes
1. Mary W. Morgan, "The Importance of One Vote," *Collier County Government Services*, revised June 29, 2000. http://www.co.collier.fl.us/elections/onevote.htm (accessed August 7, 2000). Morgan is the former supervisor of elections for Collier County, Florida.
2. Norman Cousins, *Anatomy of an Illness* (New York: Bantam Doubleday Dell, 1991), n.p.
3. Mother Teresa, Georges Gorrée and Jean Barbier, *The Love of Christ: Spiritual Counsels* (San Francisco: Harper and Row, 1982), n.p.

CHAPTER FOUR STUDY GUIDE

1. Using the DESIGN acrostic, list personal characteristics that would best identify you.

   Desire:

   Experience:

   Spiritual gift:

   Individual style:

   Growth phase:

   Natural abilities:

2. Why do you think accountability is so difficult for some people?

3. What would be the hardest tests of accountability for you?

4. Read Daniel 5:12. Daniel is said to have possessed an "extraordinary spirit." Some translations call it a "spirit of excellence." What are some of the characteristics of this kind of spirit?

CHAPTER FIVE

MINING LEADERSHIP GIFTS IN THE CHURCH

I have a dream!

MARTIN LUTHER KING, JR.

I LIVED IN JAPAN DURING MY JUNIOR HIGH SCHOOL YEARS. MY FATHER SERVED IN THE UNITED STATES ARMY, AND FOR THREE YEARS HE WAS STATIONED IN A SMALL TOWN CALLED ZAMA. WHERE WE LIVED WAS A BEAUTIFUL PLACE, BUT IT WAS STILL AN ARMY INSTALLATION ENCLOSED BY BARBED WIRE. THE BASE LOOKED LIKE ANY VINTAGE AMERICAN TOWN, BUT OUTSIDE THE FENCES WAS THE MYSTIQUE OF JAPAN. I LOOKED FORWARD TO OUR TRIPS OFF BASE AND INTO THE COUNTRYSIDE.

One summer day, all of us kids jumped into the car for a ride into the cool mountains surrounding Tokyo. We stopped at a lookout point that offered a breathtaking view of one of the lush valleys. The mountains were blanketed with cedar trees, and the valleys stretched as far as we could see, each one reaching out to a sleepy village.

We decided to stop for lunch. On one side of the road, a little Japanese woman was selling *bentos*, Japanese box lunches. On the other side, a man dressed in a traditional *yukata*, or "happy coat," caught my attention. He was selling tiny birds. He held a dozen or so bamboo cages, each one containing a small bird that resembled a finch.

"*Irrashai-mase!*" he called. "Welcome! May I help you?"

"How much for one bird?" I asked.

"100 yen each," he called back in Japanese.

In those days, 100 yen was worth about 36 cents. Such a deal! I handed the vendor a 100-yen coin, and I selected one of the bamboo cages containing a tiny finch. As I began to walk back to the car to show off my new purchase, the man called out after me.

"*Sumimasen!* (Excuse me!) Don't forget to bring the cage back when you're done!"

"Bring back the cage when I'm done?" I questioned. "I'm not planning to eat the thing. I just want to take it home as a pet."

"Oh no," he replied. "You don't understand! The bird and the cage are not for you to take home. The 100 yen is to take the bird to the edge of the valley and release it, so it will be able to fly freely!"

Quite frankly, that was about the last thing in the world I had on my mind. Release the bird I had just bought with my hard-earned money? Ridiculous! That was the dumbest thing I had ever heard. But I didn't have much of a choice in the matter. The man was keeping a close watch on me to make sure he retrieved his cage.

I guess the more I thought about it, the more novel it sounded. *Why not?* I figured it was worth a try! So I walked over to the edge of the ravine overlooking the valley below. I opened the cage door and gave the bird a couple of nudges. Edging its way suspiciously toward the door of the cage, it suddenly launched into flight with a jubilant chorus of tweets and whistles. I watched the bird fly over the valley and swirl its way back toward me as if to respectfully say "Thank you." Then it soared so high that I lost it in the sun. Within moments, the bird had disappeared.

I returned the cage to the vendor, who bowed in the gracious Japanese form. I didn't return home with a bird, but I did take with me something much greater. I learned a profound lesson that has remained with me to this day, and it later would forever change my perspective about serving people. Looking back on the experience now, I would have paid 100 times more if I knew how important that moment would be to me years later. That day I learned the precious lesson of being a dream releaser.

"TELL 'EM I DIED RICH"

The story is told of two miners who spent half their lives looking for gold in the Pacific Northwest. Under the scrutiny and criticism of the townspeople, the two miners pressed on, believing in their ability to strike it rich. These two unrelenting miners became the joke of the town, as week after week, they would return from their labors empty-handed. Nevertheless, they pressed on with a deep confidence that someday they would find what they were looking for.

One sultry afternoon, after months of painstaking digging in an old mine shaft, they finally hit pay dirt! Huge nuggets of gold were visible from a rich, undiscovered vein. Furiously, the men began pulling nugget after nugget from the grip of the earth.

No one knows whether it was a faulty support pole, the exuberance of the shouting or the gradual loosening of the dirt that caused the collapse, but the sound of loud, piercing cracks in the timber brought the two men to an abrupt halt. Suddenly the mine shaft caved in, and tons of dirt pounded both men to the floor.

One of the men lay injured on the ground, holding tightly to a nugget he had claimed. The other miner, still able to move, pulled himself up, yelling, "Come on! We've got to get out of here before the whole thing collapses! I'll help you! Get up! Leave the gold. We don't have a second to lose!"

The injured miner, still clutching the gold nugget tightly to his chest, said, "No. Just leave me here. I found what I've been looking for. I've spent my life searching for this vein, and I'm not about to let it go now. Leave me here. You go! Get out of here."

"Don't be foolish! We've gotta get you back!" his partner replied. Just then, the rafters trembled again, spilling more dirt into the dust-filled shaft. "If I leave you here, you'll surely die! What will I tell your family! What will I tell the folks back in town?"

The badly injured miner wheezed his final words between strained coughs, as dust filled the collapsing chamber.

"Just tell 'em I died rich," he whispered with a final breath. "Just tell 'em I died rich."

DREAM RELEASERS

The Church is laden with treasures, dreams and precious gifts, yet too many precious souls are going to their graves with songs left unsung, gifts yet unwrapped and dreams unreleased. Too many of God's people are dying rich! Like the Japanese finch, treasures and dreams need to be released. In every person's heart is a dream of what he or she can become for the Lord—a dream that sees them making a difference in the world, in their families and in their churches.

God calls each and every leader to be a dream releaser. There is nothing more spectacular than seeing people's dreams released and being used for the glory of God! There's just no greater joy.

That's just what Loren Cunningham did at Youth With A Mission. He released the dreams in thousands of young people's hearts to go into the mission fields, and their dreams came to pass. Through his vision and leadership, Loren mobilized scores of young evangelists who today are still bringing the good news to unreached people groups.

Mother Teresa did the same in Calcutta. God had deposited the gifts of mercy and servanthood into the hearts of thousands of willing servants; but before Mother Teresa entered the scene, those gifts lay dormant. She found a way for those dreams to be discovered, developed and deployed in reaching the poorest of the poor in Calcutta.

We all have dreams in our hearts just waiting to be released. These gifts, if mobilized and aligned toward a common, God-glorifying purpose, can transform any congregation into a powerful army for the Lord.

BUILDING A LEADERSHIP BASE

May I offer a word to pastors and leaders? One of the most critical keys to doing church as a team is to build an ever-increasing core of servant-leaders. You were not designed to do church alone. You are not a one-man band. No one is. It's no fun trying to play all the instruments yourself and sing, too!

Let me illustrate it this way. Imagine that I hold out before you a one- square-foot piece of cardboard, and onto it I slowly empty a bucket of white sand. The sand will accumulate, and as it does, a pyramid of sand will form. Now what will happen if I pour another bucket of sand onto the cardboard? The amount of sand will increase until the cardboard can hold no more. So what will happen to the excess sand if I keep pouring? That's right. It will overflow the edges and cascade onto the floor. The cardboard base can only hold so much.

Now what if I empty, not just another bucket, but a whole barrel of sand onto your cardboard? Will it hold any more? Obviously not! Forgive my pressing of the issue, but now I am going to back a truckload of sand into the room and dump it. Now does your cardboard hold more sand? No! (But the floor is now a mess.)

What do we have to do to hold more sand? You've got it. We have to expand the base!

The leadership in any church can be likened to that piece of cardboard: The larger the base, the more sand you can hold. If your leadership base is small, it doesn't matter how much sand you pour onto it. It will be impossible for you to hold any more sand—until you increase the size of the base! That's the secret to what many churches call closing the back door. Some church leaders feel as if their doors are turnstiles through which people come in but never stay. Visitors can't seem to become part of the life of the church, so they leave. Increasing the leadership base by building a solid core of leaders is primary to a church's foundation for the future.

The first step in building a core of leaders is to believe that they are there. You must believe that God would never call a leader to oversee a ministry without providing everything necessary for its fruitfulness and success! Many pastors and ministers have the best reason in the world for why things just aren't happening like they should at their churches: "We have no leaders!" But God is not so cruel as to call you to build an ark without providing the necessary materials for its completion.

*God will provide all you need to fulfill what
He has called your church to do.*

God will provide all you need to fulfill what He has called your church to do. But first, you must believe that the leaders are there. Why? Because they are! Look for them. Find them. They might be right under your nose, but if you are not looking for them, you'll never see them.

If I am looking for my shoes, but I don't believe that they are in the closet, then I won't look there. Likewise, if I don't believe that there are great potential leaders in my church, I won't look there to find them!

GOD HAS ALREADY PROVIDED

In Exodus 15:22-26, we find the children of Israel making the first of many complaints after being delivered from bondage in Egypt. They have crossed the Red Sea and traveled inland until they ran out of water. The hot sands of the Sinai are baking the

Israelites until they are parched and thirsty. After a few miles, they come upon a small lake, but the water is bitter and unfit to drink. Like the bitterness of the lake, anger, grumbling and disgust are unleashed against Moses and Aaron, as the people cry, "What shall we drink?"

Then Scripture gives us a beautiful gem for every leader:

> Then he cried out to the LORD, and the LORD showed him a tree; and he threw it into the waters, and the waters became sweet (Exod. 15:25).

Moses cried out to the Lord, and when he did, God showed him a tree. Now read this portion again, and you will discover that God didn't create a tree then and there for Moses to find it. The tree had always been there! God just showed it to him.

Moses and Aaron must have walked by that tree dozens of times without ever recognizing its potential! The people may have eaten lunch under that very same tree. They probably even complained from under the shade of that tree.

The people were complaining because God hadn't provided an answer to their dilemma: extreme thirst in the desert heat. Yet all the while, their answer was right under their noses! (Or, rather, right above their heads.) But because they were too busy complaining about what they didn't have, their eyes were blinded to what they *did* have! So many of God's people through the ages have been so preoccupied with what God had not provided for them that they were oblivious to the wondrous gifts He *had* given them.

Let God show you the tree. It's there, and so are your leaders. You may be having lunch with them this week! You may be fellowshipping with them today, but you will never be able to see them until you believe that they are there.

YOU GOTTA BELIEVE THEY'RE THERE!

A dear pastor friend and I were talking over lunch one day. He was having trouble finding quality leaders in his church. He was on the verge of burnout from undertaking many of the ministry responsibilities himself.

"If I had a bigger church," he observed, "there would be more leaders to choose from. But right now there just aren't any!"

My reply to him came in the form of a question. "When you look at a forest, what do you see?" I asked.

"Elementary, Watson," he quipped. "Trees!"

"That's your problem," I replied. "All you see are trees. You've got to see more than trees. You've got to see the houses!"

I could tell that he wasn't quite tracking with me.

"Let me explain," I continued. "When I look at a forest, I see houses. I see beautiful dressers, rocking chairs, bed frames, cabinets and desks! They're all in the forest, and they're beautiful!"

From the look on his face, I could see he was beginning to reevaluate our friendship or at least question the benefit our having lunch together. But before he could jump to any premature conclusions, I hastened to my point.

"No, you won't find them already completed. But the potential is all there! Sure, you'll still have to cut and sand and varnish the wood, but it's all there. Everything you need to furnish your entire home is in that forest. You just need to see more than trees in order to be motivated to harvest the wood. You have to see their potential! You gotta believe there's gold in them thar hills if you're gonna muster up the energy you need to mine it out!"

When you believe that they are there, you'll be surprised at how many wonderful leaders start showing up!

CHAPTER FIVE STUDY GUIDE

1. List three dreams you have tucked away in your heart that have yet to come true.

   a.

   b.

   c.

2. What factors are hindering each one from coming to pass?

   a.

   b.

   c.

3. What are some of the reasons we fail to see our own potential?

4. What are some of the reasons we fail to see other people's potential?

DEVELOPING SERVANT-LEADERS

*Give me one hundred preachers who fear nothing but sin
and desire nothing but God, and I care not a straw whether
they be clergymen or laymen, such alone will shake the gates
of hell and set up the kingdom of God upon earth.*

JOHN WESLEY, 1703-1791

O NE OF THE GREATEST ROLES OF A PASTOR IS TO BELIEVE IN THE PEOPLE UNDER HIS CARE. THIS ONE QUALITY ALONE CAN DO MORE TO DEVELOP EMERGING LEADERS IN A CHURCH THAN ANY CLASS OR GROUP STUDY. WE ALL NEED SOMEONE TO BELIEVE IN US, TO SEE THE BEST IN US AND TO HELP US BRING IT FORTH! SURE, WE MAY HAVE MANY FAULTS THAT STILL NEED TO BE CORRECTED, BUT WHAT WE NEED ARE PEOPLE WHO WILL LOOK BEYOND OUR GLITCHES TO SEE GOD'S BEST.

In Mark 2, we find a story about Jesus seeing the best in people. The story opens with four zealous friends of a paralytic man, whom we'll call Reuben. The friends have heard talk of a carpenter from Nazareth who is teaching at Peter's house in Capernaum. Now, a visiting teacher is not all that unique; guest rabbis often taught in the neighborhood synagogues. But what catches the attention of these four friends are reports of Jesus healing sick and hurting people, and they think of their friend Reuben.

That evening, with their friend on a stretcher, they begin the journey to Peter's house. However, the weight and awkwardness of the load delays their arrival. By the time they reach the home, a crowd has filled the living room and overflowed into the backyard, leaving no room for latecomers.

Refusing to have their hopes dashed, the most creative among them comes up with a risky idea. "I know what we can do!" he says. "Let's climb up on the roof and make a hole! You heard me. Make a hole! Then we can let Reuben down on the stretcher right in front of Jesus! That'll get His attention, won't it?" Without wasting any time, the four friends clamber onto the roof with ol' Reuben in tow, and they proceed to execute Plan A with a passion!

I have no idea where they mustered up such courage! There was such a sense of urgency that they didn't even stop to calculate what the repair bill would be for Peter's roof. If they had known the reputation of this rough fisherman and his volatile outbursts, I doubt that they would have carried out their scheme.

Nevertheless, poor Reuben soon lay helplessly dangling in front of the guest speaker. Above, four pairs of eyes curiously gazed through the newly crafted skylight. The room fell into an uncomfortable silence, as everyone held their breath, awaiting the reprimand of the Master. After all, what would the scribes think? What would the Law demand? Would the Teacher chide the zealous, unthinking friends? Would He demand they immediately undertake repairs to Peter's roof?

Jesus' response holds for us a leadership principle that is worth a pound of gold. Instead of chastising the zealous friends for their ill-planned exploit, He looks straight at them, and the Bible captures the moment with these words:

> And Jesus *seeing their faith* said to the paralytic, "My son, your sins are forgiven" (Mark 2:5, emphasis added).

Jesus could have chided them for their extreme measures or lack of preplanning. He could have pointed out their tardiness due to their own procrastination and late departure. Instead, He saw their faith! He saw the action of Reuben's friends for what it was and called it faith.

A LEADER SEES WHAT'S BEST

Look for faith in those around you. Look for evidence of God's presence, not evidence of His absence. In each of us is a measure of faith, a desire for God's best. Every person has a yearning to do well, to make a difference. God created us that way! Those dreams may yet be inside each every person in your church, though they may be somewhat fragile.

You may even notice novice attempts to fly, to get those dreams off the ground. Sometimes those attempts may resemble the dance of a disoriented albatross more than the takeoff of an F-22 fighter jet. But encourage them, even if the plane fails to make it off the tarmac. See the faith and the heart behind what they're attempting to do. While the execution of those dreams may still require further development, the potential that remains inside each of us is a precious commodity to God! See your people through the eyes of Jesus and watch! You'll begin to see miracles increase in your church and a corresponding decrease in justifications for why they are not happening.

Some of the greatest discoveries come about when people readjust their eyes to see what's best about a situation rather than what's worst. I heard a story about George De Mestral walking his dog one afternoon when the dog got loose for a moment and ran off through some tall grass. When George finally retrieved his wayward pet, the dog was covered with burrs tangled in his fur. When he arrived home, George could have cursed the dog while cutting the burrs out. Instead, he curiously took a cutting of the fur and viewed it under his microscope. Amazed at the gripping characteristics of the burrs, he studied them further. George's curiosity and his willingness to see the potential in a sticky situation ultimately led him to invent Velcro!

HOW TO PLEASE GOD

Let me make a disclaimer here. As wonderful as it is to have leaders who believe in us, in the final analysis, it is the responsibility of each and every person to develop his or her own gifts. Jesus gave us a clear teaching on investing what God has entrusted to us:

And the one also who had received the one talent came up and said, "Master, I knew you to be a hard man. . . . I was afraid, and went away and hid your talent in the ground; see, you have what is yours." But his master answered and said to him, "You wicked, lazy slave, you knew that I reap where I did not sow, and gather where I scattered no seed. Then you ought to have put my money in the bank, and on my arrival I would have received my money back with interest. Therefore take away the talent from him, and give it to the one who has the ten talents. For to everyone who has shall more be given, and he shall have an abundance; but from the one who does not have, even what he does have shall be taken away" (Matt. 25:24-29).

I have heard many applications of this story, but one message rings true: You can't please God by not investing what you have been given! We must use our gifts, not bury them. I would rather risk all for God and come up short than to never make the attempt.

DEVELOPING YOUR GIFTS BY TAKING A RISK

Leaders develop their gifts by considering the consequences and going for it anyway. There are no shortcuts. If it's for God, don't ask, Why? Ask, Why not?

Jesus tells us that we cannot please God by playing it safe. Are you willing to risk what you have for the sake of the Master? Too many of us are afraid, so we bury our gifts, and we wonder why we never grow or increase in our giftedness and influence. One of the keys to the success of the Early Church was that they were men and women who "risked their lives for the name of our Lord Jesus Christ" (Acts 15:26).

One of my favorite Bible verses is Proverbs 14:4: "Where no oxen are, the manger is clean, but much increase comes by the strength of the ox." In other words, strength will always bring with it problems, but that's normal! Don't be afraid of making mistakes. If your goal is to keep a clean manger, then you won't need (or want) any oxen. But if your desire is to make a difference with your life, then you need to be ready and willing to clean up a few piles of doo-doo.

You see, if you're afraid of messes, if you're afraid of failing, if you're afraid of risking, you'll never get anywhere. As a baseball man once said, you can't steal second base with your foot still on first. You've got to be willing to venture off the bag, take the lead and go for it!

In Hawaii, we often hear advertisements beckoning potential travelers to Las Vegas for a weekend of gambling. The fares are very reasonable, and hotel rooms are available at bargain prices. Of course, the plan is to lure you to drop your hard-earned dollars at the roulette tables or watch them disappear into one of the many one-armed bandits that line the casinos. Each year, millions flock to these hollow promised lands to risk their savings in hopes of striking it rich. We think nothing of taking risks with our money, even though we know there is a far greater chance of returning home empty-handed than there is of returning a millionaire.

C. T. Studd, a great preacher and missionary of yesteryear, once said, "The gamblers for gold are so many, but the gamblers for God are so few. Where are the gamblers for God?"

We risk our lives each time we fly in an airplane. We take a risk when we invest in a stock. We take a risk when we get married. We take a risk when we buy a house. I think it's high time we take a risk for God! He's so much more worthy (and secure) than any earthly investment.

I remember a little poem that reminds me that life is about taking risks:

There once lived a man who never risked,
He never tried.

He never laughed,
He never cried.
Then one day, when he passed away,
His insurance was denied.
They said since he never really lived,
Then he never really died!
—Anonymous

You can develop your gifts only by using them. Sure, you may be required to take some risks—the risk of making a mistake, the risk of faltering or stammering if you speak, even the risk of failure. Go for it anyway! Don't wait until your gifts are fully developed

Gifts don't ripen like a bunch of bananas when put in a dark place.
Gifts that are hidden away only get rotten.

before you put them to use. That just won't happen, because gifts don't ripen like a bunch of bananas put in a dark place. Gifts that are hidden away don't ripen; they get rotten!

"TAKE ME OUT TO THE BALL GAME!"

For example, let's say that during a revival campaign, you received the gift of, well, er, the ability to play professional baseball. (Just for the sake of dialogue, mind you.) Hands were laid on your head, and this rare and wonderful gift was bestowed on you. But even though the gift is now in you, you still look the same, act the same and walk the same. So what do you have to do to see this gift come to pass? What must you do in order for it to blossom and mature? You have to play baseball!

So you put on a uniform and go to the ballpark. You've never even swung a bat before. The coach steps to the pitcher's mound and you to the plate. He throws the first pitch, and you swing with all your might—and miss it by a mile. You fall mightily. Do you quit now? No! You stagger to stand, dust yourself off and take another pitch.

The coach encourages you. "It's in you! Swing again. I know it's in you!" So you take your stance in the batter's box, and the second pitch comes whizzing by and smacks into the catcher's glove. You didn't even see it go by! "It's in you," the coach says again. "Swing the bat next time. Swing the bat!"

The third pitch is hurled. You close your eyes and swing with everything you've got.

KABOOM!

The ball rockets off the sweet spot of your Louisville Slugger and sails into the outfield.

"That's it!" shouts the coach. "I knew you had it in you. Keep it up, now. Keep it up!"

As the months go by, you continue training. The balls are going further and further. And when you take the field at shortstop, nothing gets by you. You're turning double plays and then triple plays! You begin to love this sport! Every day, you can be found on the baseball diamond, fielding grounders or hitting home runs.

Now fast-forward about three years. Your reputation as a promising rookie has spread, and a couple of scouts from the

Atlanta Braves fly in to see one of your games. They watch you hit, field and run the bases like a pro. In the fourth inning, you turn a spectacular double play, and one scout leans over to the other and remarks, "Now, *that* kid has a gift. He has a gift!"

And he's right, but how did your gift become developed? How did it come to its fullness?

You had to play the game!

This principle applies to doing church as a team. You must use your gift! Even though you miss a few grounders or drop the occasional pop-up, stay in there. I know it's in you because God put it there! When you strike out, get in there and swing again.

Say yes more often than you say no. Get involved. If after a while, you find your piece of the puzzle just doesn't fit, simply move to another position, but keep serving! Pretty soon you'll be dazzling them in the field and knocking the ball out of the park, and people will look at you and exclaim, "Wow! You are so gifted! How did that happen?"

And you'll reply, "I just played baseball."

BUILDING YOUR CHARACTER BEFORE BUILDING YOUR MINISTRY

When I was a relatively new Christian, I taught several morning Bible studies to a group of seven or eight men. We often met at restaurants, where we would pore over the Scriptures and pour coffee into us for an hour or so before going to work. Looking back, I recall that I learned more from teaching than I ever gave out. I think that God had me teach those studies not so much for what would happen *through* me as much as what would happen *in* me. You see, God is less interested in what you're *doing* and more interested in what you're *becoming*.

As I look back over the years, I recall many times when my involvement in something had little to do with what I could contribute but a lot more to do with God building my character! Sometimes the Lord will place you in a position for a season because He knows there are some things that need to be developed inside you. When you get involved, God will instill character or virtue in you through the process—perhaps endurance, submission, people skills or positive attitudes.

Here is a letter from a book I wrote to my children called *Gems Along The Way*:

Dear Amy, Aaron and Abby,

I saw a lady's four-carat diamond ring the other day. Wow! Was that ever impressive! The diamond must have been worth $20,000! (I'm not a diamond appraiser or anything, but after considering it for a moment, I felt strongly that such a diamond would surely detract from the natural beauty of your mother's hand, so I didn't buy it.)

Anyway, the gold band was a simple one, with a few smaller diamonds on either side. Holding the diamond in place was a setting that included maybe five or six prongs.

"My!" I thought. "That setting had better be strong! It's holding on to $20,000!"

Although the setting doesn't get as much attention as the diamond itself, it is equally as important. Any wise jeweler would never put such a precious jewel in a poor or weak setting. If he did, then one small bump and the gem would be lost! The strength and quality of the setting will determine the security and staying power of the gem!

Character is like that setting. God has promised us such wonderful gems! Yet without the basis of character, His promises would be lost or forfeited at the first bump! The Holy Spirit's desire is to produce character in each of us prior to the setting of the gems. Whether those gems are marriage, an influential position, a ministry, finances or a family, each of these will require character. This is the setting that needs to be developed prior to the placement of the gem.

Strengthen your setting. Build your character. Learn to forgive, to be diligent, to be honest. Learn to stay steady and faithful, to keep commitments, to go by what you know and not necessarily by what you feel.

Here's a simple definition of character that I heard along the way: Character is the ability to follow through on a worthy decision long after the emotion of making that decision has passed.

God will refine your metal until it's pure gold. He will shape your character until it's strong and trustworthy. Then when God sees that the setting is ready, He will be faithful to place His very best gems in your life! That's when you'll shine!

Love,
Dad

Over the long haul, ministry should charge you up. You'll build character along the way, but if week after week you come away from ministry drained, then stop! Reevaluate what may be causing this and find a remedy. Don't keep running on empty! Sometimes it may be God working on your character, and sometimes it may be time for you to move. Either is fine. Just be sure that if you move, you are always following the leading of the Lord and not running from a problem.

In the past, I have experienced overwhelming feelings on the job that had nothing to do with my placement. They had more to do with my character development than with my gifts or passion. What we often define as burnout may actually be the result of personality conflicts or a problem with submission to authority. These are character issues that God wants to deal with once and for all! If we bail out, the lesson will only have to be repeated in another setting—second verse, same as the first.

This is where accountability through friendships has become a lifesaver for me. I need people watching out for me, and I need to do the same for others. Develop relationships along the way that are deep enough that you are willing to allow these friends to speak into your life. Being committed to one another's success is essential for doing church as a team. If we could do that for each other (you may sing this next line), what a wonderful world this would be!

SECURITY CHECKPOINT

Developing servant-leaders requires one major ingredient: security. Pastors, if you are not secure as a leader, you will find it virtually impossible to attract, develop or retain other leaders. You cannot do church as a team while battling insecurity. Good leaders must be able to build confidence in others.

Secure people encourage others and enjoy their successes. They can appreciate and applaud the achievements of those they have put into positions to succeed. Secure leaders are neither territorial nor possessive. They are willing and able to surround themselves with people more qualified than themselves.

Insecure people, on the other hand, feel that if they are not controlling everything around them, then they are not doing their job. They fear criticism and they worry about what others think. Such people can never believe that others are competent enough to do the job. Hence, they seldom delegate anything at all! Leaders must always remember that everyone will make mistakes and that mistakes are often the best classrooms in the world.

Take a look at yourself as a leader. You will do well and score high if you catch people doing things right and show a genuine excitement for their accomplishments. It is well said that we would be surprised how much can be accomplished when we don't care who gets the credit!

Take a look at this 10-point checklist and see how you fare:

A secure leader	An insecure leader
Encourages others' attempts	Sabotages others' efforts
Points out others' strong points	Brings attention to others' faults
Overlooks flaws	Uses others' flaws as ammunition
Readily admits own mistakes	Is defensive and justifies mistakes
Gives away credit to others	Demands or manipulates credit
Rejoices when others succeed	Is jealous of others' successes
Is excited when others do it better	Is easily intimidated
Is willing to risk to improve	Plays it safe to retain position
Is content to remain anonymous	Requires others to notice
Is quick to build teams	Wants to do things himself

What kind of leader are you? How did you score? Are you someone who enjoys catching your people doing something right? Can you easily give credit away and show genuine excitement at the accomplishments of others? How hard is it for you to build a team? Let's take a look at how these things can be done in today's church.

PASSING BATONS

As you read through the Gospels, you will notice something interesting about the leadership style of Jesus: He began passing batons to His disciples early in His ministry. By the sixth chapter of Mark, He is already choosing a dozen men to succeed Him! Just as in a relay race, passing the baton in ministry isn't meant to be a sudden last-ditch effort. Plan on it. Start passing batons early in your ministry.

When I began studying the early missionary efforts to Hawaii, Titus Coan became one of my heroes, as did Hiram Bingham. These men served the people of Hawaii during the early and middle 1800s. Now, Coan and Bingham did hundreds of things right in reaching the Hawaiian islands, but they also made two costly mistakes that hindered the future of their ministries.

Their first mistake was allowing their second generation to be lost—their own children grew up without a deep and genuine faith. There may have been many reasons for this, but suffice to say the missionaries' plates were so full that they probably had little time left for their own children. That is a poignant lesson for all of us.

The second costly mistake I noticed was that these men passed the baton too late in life. Just before his death, Titus Coan passed the mantle of leadership to a few potential leaders. They carried on as best they could but, inevitably, the mission diminished and the vision faded.

It may take only a moment to pass a baton, but it takes much longer to pass the heart of that baton. When doing church as a team, passing out batons early ensures that no one burns out and that we all share the joys (and sorrows) together. At New Hope, we don't pass batons as a precursor to the end of one's ministry. We pass batons as a way of including others in the race!

You don't pass the baton in a relay race when you are already pooped out! You pass it at the very apex of your stride. The same is true in doing church as a team. Invite others into your ministry. Pass batons. Include new people, and don't be intimidated when others do it better! God will always have a place for you, and the greater a servant you are, the greater the joy you'll experience. If your gift is to build platforms for other emerging leaders, when they are successful, you will be called to build more!

One of the fastest and easiest ways to pass batons is through shadowing. Shadowing is simply following someone around who has been serving in an area of interest to you. It is a way of introducing new people into a ministry, and we recommend this approach in almost every volunteer ministry at New Hope. It's a low-risk orientation that gives budding "ministers" a glimpse of what is being done and how. It's also an opportunity for everyone to build new friendships along the way!

The three stages of shadowing are

Stage 1—I do. You watch.

Stage 2—We do together.

Stage 3—You do. I applaud!

When my daughter Amy was a senior in high school, she ran on the relay team in track. I watched as the team practiced one thing again and again. They would all line up, facing the same direction, about an arm's length apart from each other. Then, while running in place, they would practice passing the baton from one runner to the other. When the baton was passed from the back to the front, they repeated the process until the passes were perfect. The reason? In a relay, the race is either won or lost in the passing of the baton.

PASSING OUT BATONS AND RUNNING TOGETHER

Passing the baton is a function of our willingness to allow God to use us fully in ministry. Answering our call and using our gifts includes being led by the Holy Spirit to help others become successful! This is part of what it means to do church as a team.

Unlike a relay team, however, you pass batons to *all* the team members. Then you run together! You don't pass a baton and then quit. You stay with the team, and you run in unison. I guess this would be better described as passing out batons.

When we look at the larger picture of God's plan for the church in a community, we can see that passing out batons is crucial. Building a team that runs together is important. Learn to pass out batons, and do it early. Don't wait until the end. Invite others into your area of ministry and readily applaud their successes. Fight the tendency to become territorial or possessive. That will only wreak havoc and discourage new and emerging leaders. An open invitation to get involved is crucial for developing an atmosphere of growth and teamwork. Passing out batons allows each of us to begin by first serving one another. Have you ever wondered why Jesus sent out His disciples two by two? I believe it was because He knew that the gospel would best be seen and understood in the context of relationships. As people witnessed the love, friendship and camaraderie of the two messengers, this gave credence to the message!

START BY SERVING EACH OTHER

Although serving the Lord and others is best done in teams, one of the ways to make this happen is by first serving the others on your team! Some call this *lateral serving,* in which serving one another is given equal importance with serving to get something accomplished. This is the esprit de corps of a church.

Lateral serving is the opposite of the attitude that says "That's not my ministry" or "That's not my responsibility." It's a willingness to occasionally do someone else's job and do it with great joy. It is seeing a task that has been overlooked by others and gratefully filling in. I have heard lateral serving described as "the art of making good on someone else's mistake."

In doing church as a team, we have learned the importance of "cross training"—training outside our specialties so we can step up and step in when others need a break or they simply need our support. Everyone has times when their flame dwindles, and that's when we need each other the most.

Someone once said that you never diminish the flame of your own candle by lighting the flame of someone else.

I like that.

CHAPTER SIX STUDY GUIDE

1. List three of the greatest fears that people have about getting involved in ministry.

   a.

   b.

   c.

2. What remedies can you give that would dispel each of these fears?

   a.

   b.

   c.

3. Often we find that God is less interested in what you are doing and more interested with what you are becoming. Make a list of some godly character qualities you have learned along the way. Can you remember specific circumstances that helped you to develop these qualities?

4. List and discuss some of the fears people have in allowing others to be included in ministry.

SETTING YOUR COMPASS

Teach me Thy way, O LORD, and lead me in a level path.

P S A L M   2 7 : 1 1

IN LEWIS CARROLL'S CLASSIC ALICE'S ADVENTURES IN WONDERLAND, YOUNG ALICE ENCOUNTERS THE CHESHIRE CAT DURING HER HURRIED ATTEMPT TO FIND HER WAY THROUGH A MAZE OF A FAIRY-TALE FOREST.

"Would you tell me, please, which way I ought to go from here?" Alice cries.

"That depends a good deal on where you want to get to," the grinning Cat answers.

"I don't much care where—" a lost and flustered Alice says.

"Then it doesn't matter which way you go," says the Cat, who soon thereafter vanishes—all except for its toothy grin.[1]

Many people, ministries and churches today feel as though they are staring at an enemy who is invisible except for a certain Cheshire Cat grin. They've lost their sense of direction, so in the midst of their confused scampering, they look to different resources—conferences, audiotape series, the newest leadership book—to find answers. And although these may be helpful for a season, there's still a nagging sense that something isn't quite right, that they're still missing the target. (It's always easier to *imitate* than it is to *incarnate*, especially during a dry season when, as in 1 Samuel 3:1, a word from the Lord is rare and visions are infrequent.) Exhausted from trying to implement the techniques that have worked for "successful" churches, they feel defeated. Oh, their hearts are right. In fact, their hearts are desperately seeking after God's best. And like Alice in Wonderland, they cry out, "Which way do I go?"

Reaching an ultimate goal means starting at the right place, and that means knowing where you're going. Before you build a house, you need a blueprint. Before a plane leaves the tarmac, the pilot must file his flight plan with the tower. Before you do church as a team, there must be a clear and concise understanding of the mission and assignment the Lord has given specifically to your local church. This is what we are referring to here as *setting your compass* and what is commonly called *vision*.

Your vision is the goal God has set for your life and for your ministry. And a clear vision provides the direction you seek for your ministry and your church. With a vision set firmly in place, there's no scampering and no confusion. Your compass is set, and your every step can be sure.

Each church has its own community, purpose, culture, passion and gifts. And because of the unique blend of all of these components, your church will have a very unique vision. The first step, catching the vision, is absolutely critical—especially for pastors. There are no shortcuts on this one.

God has a very special, tailor-made vision for your church, just as He has one tailor-made for you! This vision will become the very foundation of your ministry, the direction for your planning and the reason for your existence. By keeping this vision clearly fixed, you will have a much better chance of fulfilling His purposes.

This is one of the most important aspects of doing church as a team: setting your compass through vision.

WHAT IS A VISION?

A sculptor named Gutzon Borglum is credited with creating the magnificent carving of Abraham Lincoln at the Lincoln Memorial in Washington, DC. He chipped the entire sculpture from one very large stone in his studio. The story is told of a cleaning lady who swept up for Borglum every day after he worked on the statue. Many months passed, and the moment of the unveiling finally arrived. Gutzon Borglum invited his faithful cleaning lady to the inaugural showing as his personal guest. As the velvet drape was drawn back, the room was filled with the sounds of awestruck admirers. The beauty of this work was stunning. Smooth lines, the clear features of Lincoln's face, the jutting jaw and pronounced cheekbones all expressed the touch of a master artist.

The evening came to a close with the artist and the cleaning woman gazing at the finished piece of art that would adorn the capitol for generations to come. "Well, what do you think?" the sculptor asked. After a brief moment, the faithful worker calmly replied, "I have only one question. How did you know that Mr. Lincoln was in that rock?"

Vision is the ability to see what others may not. It is the capacity to see potential—what things could be. Vision is the ability to see what God sees and the God-given motivation to bring what you see to pass! Whether it is a personal vision or a vision for a church, vision is what stirs up faith! You can't have one without the other. Faith will birth vision, and a vision will fuel your faith.

Hebrews 11:1 describes that kind of vision: "Faith is the assurance of things hoped for, the conviction of things not seen." Faith is required to see the unseen, and by seeing what God has in store for your future, you begin to have vision. This means seeing not only with your eyes but also with your heart.

Stephen Covey, in his best-selling book *The Seven Habits of Highly Effective People*, talks about beginning with the end in mind. He based this on the principle that everything has been created twice—once in the realm of imagination, where only you can see it, and then in the physical realm, where everyone else can see it.[2] When you can conceive a clear picture of what God's blueprint is for your life or that of the church, you have vision! The clearer the picture, the more likely others are to catch the same vision. When everyone catches the vision, it becomes more than a vision; it becomes a reality.

What can you believe God for? Much of your future will depend on your answer to this one question. Jesus Himself illustrated the importance of a person's answer:

> As Jesus left the house, he was followed by two blind men crying out, "Mercy, Son of David! Mercy on us!" When Jesus got home, the blind men went in with him. Jesus said to them, "Do you really believe I can do this?" They said, "Why, yes, Master!" He touched their eyes and said, *"Become what you believe."* It happened. They saw (Matt. 9:27-30, *THE MESSAGE*, emphasis added).

We become what we believe. If you can't believe that God will do something wonderful in your life, you will have what you believe. If you can believe, what miracles will come to pass before your eyes!

I play the guitar. Not well, mind you, but I love the *sound* of the guitar. I have for years. One day when I was living in Eugene, Oregon, I was invited by my guitar teacher to listen to a great jazz guitarist. This man produced the most beautiful, melodic lines I had ever heard. I was in awe of how his skilled fingers moved with such ease and clarity. I turned to my teacher and said, "Man, I could never play like that!"

He turned to me and, as if to add emphasis to his words, slowly replied "That's why you don't. You can't believe that you could do it. And you won't until you can *change your mind!*"

One man says, "I can." Another says, "I can't."

Which man is correct?

Both.

Scripture says, "For as [a man] thinks in his heart, so is he" (Prov. 23:7, *NKJV*). It's as simple as that. Whatever we envision for ourselves in our hearts and minds becomes what we see in our lives.

Great vision, therefore, calls for the ability to see as God sees. It requires faith, but that's only one important element of vision, for vision begins in the seedbed of dreams.

IT'S NEVER TOO LATE TO START DREAMING

Dream lofty dreams, and as you dream, so shall you become. Your vision is the promise of what you shall one day be! — James Allen

The first step in finding your vision is to dream. That's right! God loves dreamers. Dreamers bring about the changes our world so desperately needs. God uses dreamers to turn dying churches into vibrant communities of excited, effective people.

God taught Abraham how to dream. He took Abraham outside of his tent and said, "Now look toward the heavens, and count the stars, if you are able to count them. . . . So shall your descendants be"; when Abraham caught the vision and believed, God commended him and "reckoned it to him as righteousness" (Gen. 15:5,6). God wanted Abraham to have a clear picture of the end result of His promise. If Abraham should catch that vision, he would be able to see it come to pass in this world.

God's heart never changes, He still wants His children to catch clear pictures of the end results of His promises. He understands that in order for us to be it, we have to see it. And by faith, we catch sight of God's foresight.

In Joel 2:28, God lets us in on one aspect of the Holy Spirit's ministry to us in the last days:

And it will come about after this that I will pour out My Spirit on all mankind; and your sons and daughters will prophesy, your old men will dream dreams, your young men will see visions.

Zero in with me on the phrase "your old men will dream dreams." There can be several applications for this promise, but let me suggest just one: It's never too late to start dreaming again!

Many in the Church have stopped dreaming, and without dreamers there can be no visionaries. Nothing changes until someone starts to dream. Some of you reading this might think that it's too late, that you'll never amount to anything. I have good news for you! One of the very reasons the Holy Spirit is being poured out on us as Christians in these days is *so we can dream again!*

A church will never outgrow its vision, and no vision will ever exceed the church leaders' ability to dream. So dream big dreams for God! One of the reasons many Christians lose motivation is that we, as believers, have stopped dreaming about the wonderful things God can do for our churches, our families and our futures.

When Disney World in Orlando opened some years ago, the widow of the great entrepreneur stood with one of the engineers of the expansive entertainment center, gazing at its magnificence and beauty. The engineer, in a genuine effort to honor one of our country's greatest innovators, turned toward Mrs. Disney and remarked, "Boy, I wish Walt could have seen this!" Without taking her eyes off the sprawling playland, she replied, "He did. That's why it's here."

God wants us to start dreaming again. That's the beginning of God-glorifying vision. Dream up the best you can for your life. If you are a pastor, dream up the best vision you can for the church. Fast-forward the tape of your mind 10 years down the road. If there were no restrictions whatsoever, what could you see for your church? Make the dream as lofty as you can. Even if it seems outrageous, fix it in your mind.

Got it?

Now read this verse from *The Living Bible*:

Now glory be to God who by his mighty power at work within us is able to do far more than we would ever dare to ask or even dream of—infinitely beyond our highest prayers, desires, thoughts, or hopes (Eph. 3:20).

Do you see what the Lord is saying? Go ahead, dream the biggest dreams you can, because as big as you can dream, God's dreams for you will always be bigger!

BEGIN WITH WHAT YOU HAVE

At the beginning stages, you may have the tendency to feel inadequate for the tasks ahead. You may feel ill equipped to measure up to any new vision, let alone a God-glorifying dream! But rest assured, God will always start with what you have, not with what you don't have.

We can learn a lot about developing, or casting, vision by examining how God communicated vision to His people through His servant Moses.

Moses had the incredible assignment of guiding God's people out of Egypt, through the wilderness and into the Promised Land. Got vision? Moses sure did! The survival of God's people depended on nothing less than his ability to discern and then communicate this vision.

This is such a powerful legacy, one that set into motion vision and direction for every future generation of God's children. Among the lessons we can glean from the practical instruction the Lord gave Moses in communicating His vision is to begin with what you have:

> The LORD spoke further to Moses, saying, "Make yourself two trumpets of silver, of hammered work you shall make them; and you shall use them for summoning the congregation and for having the camps set out" (Num. 10:1,2).

God said to make the trumpets of silver, but where would these recently freed slaves get their hands on precious metals? There were no jewelry stores in the neighborhood, at least not at that time. Fortunately, God had commanded the Israelites to plunder the wealth of the Egyptians prior to their departure, and they had collected numerous articles of gold and silver (see Exod. 12:35,36). All that was required was found within their grasp! The trumpets were to be made out of what they had, not from what they didn't possess.

As you begin to develop your vision, look at what you have. Look at the skills and talents, the spiritual gifts and passions God has planted in you. If you're developing a vision for your church, what precious commodities can be found within your people? God always starts with what you have. You never need to worry about implementing a vision that is beyond your grasp.

David Livingstone was one of Christendom's greatest missionaries to Africa. He not only brought the gospel to the natives of this vast continent, but he lived it as well, giving him great favor in the hearts of the people. After God called him to go deeper into the jungle to take the message of Jesus Christ to those who had never heard it, Livingstone encountered a remote tribe of the Congo. He learned that according to custom, he was to first call for an audience with the tribal chief before entering their village. Failure to comply with this custom could have cost him his life.

Livingstone was required to wait outside the village with all his possessions lined up next to him. The chief, as a sign of acceptance, would take whatever he desired from among the missionary's possessions. To complete the exchange, the chief would give the guest something of his own. Then and only then would Livingstone be authorized to enter and share the gospel.

The scene resembled an orderly garage sale. Livingstone had set out his Bible, writing pad, clothes, shoes, blanket—and his goat. Livingstone suffered from a weak stomach that required him to drink goat's milk on a daily basis. The local drinking water was often questionable, so this was his answer to survival. Often Livingstone had asked God to heal his infirmity, but it seemed he was sentenced to drinking goat's milk every morning.

After what seemed an eternity to Livingstone, the chief emerged from his tent and made his way slowly toward the man of God whom he had heard much about. Ornately attired in ivory and gold, the chief was followed closely by his advisors and priests. He surveyed the possessions of the missionary, while Livingstone silently prayed, *Lord, let him take anything he wants except my goat! You know I need its milk for my very survival. Lord, blind his eyes to the goat!*

The chief promptly walked over to the goat and pointed at it, and one of his advisors whisked the animal away! Livingstone stood stunned, as if his life had abruptly come to a halt.

A few moments later, the man who took his goat returned. In exchange, he handed Livingstone a stick and left. "A stick?!" the man of God cried. "Ridiculous! Here, he takes my life's sustenance, and in return I get an old stick!"

A man standing close by, seeing Livingstone's confusion, quickly spoke. "Oh no! That is not a stick. My friend, that is the chief's very own scepter. With it, you will gain entry to every tribe and village in the interior. You have been given safe passage and great authority as a gift from the king!"

Then Livingstone realized what God had done. From that time forward, God's Word spread to thousands and thousands of native people. And, as a side note, Livingstone's stomach ailment was healed, too.

God never asks for more than we are able to handle, though there will be times when it will be beyond what we are *able* to do. The difference is faith. God can bridge the difference; that's not the issue. The issue is what you have faith for. In the case of vision, be of great faith! Possess a confident assurance of the things you hope for, convinced beyond your comprehension and beyond circumstances that He is in motion to fulfill them for you. Begin with what you have, faithful that God will fulfill the rest.

BLOW A CLEAR TRUMPET

Let's get back to Moses. Notice that God commanded Moses to "make yourself" these trumpets (Num. 10:1). He was not to buy them, rent them or borrow them from a local marching band. He was to hammer them out for himself and then learn to blow them until they sounded clearly. The trumpets would be used to call the congregation together, to summon the leaders, to warn the people and to bring organization to their travel plans when God told them to move.

Once He gives you a God-glorifying dream of what your ministry can be, the next step is to hammer it out. Yes, you'll catch a clear picture of His promise, but a critical step is hammering out the details of how that dream will become reality. This step is probably the most time-consuming and the most important. This is where you begin laying out a clear path, or blueprint, for the future.

Hammering out the details requires the ability to see where a church is (point A) and where the church is going (point B), as well as how to take it from point A to point B. For example, let's say New Hope has a weekly attendance of about 6,000 members.

This is our point A. Our vision may be that in three or four years, we should be at 10,000. That's point B. Next we need to hammer out a trumpet to produce that clear call.

In this case, we would need to have facilities that can hold and serve 10,000 people at a time. We'll also need to beef up our Front Lines ministry, which produces our weekend services, so that our services continue to be inviting and alive. For that to happen we have to have good administration and strong internal communications; the leader with the vision must project a clear goal to the congregation; and so forth. We'll also need to establish a greater platform of volunteer leaders, one that grows proportionately with the size of the church. That way we don't burn anybody out.

Then we make sure that our discipleship program is effective so that when new people get saved, they will immediately be nurtured in a discipleship group. That means we'll have to bolster our small-group ministry, since we're a church of small groups and that's how we meet the needs of the people. When everybody is in a small group, there is connectedness.

That's what it's going to take to make this goal become a reality. In order to have a functioning church of 10,000 members in the future, we'll have to set up the infrastructure for it today.

When city planners first thought of building a freeway in Hawaii, the proposal was met with hysterics. Nobody took it seriously. Most people could not see the need for a three-lane highway connecting the then-small town of Honolulu to the rest of the island. There were very few car owners on the island, and they had little reason to leave their countryside homes and businesses to come into town. Today, Hawaii's population has rocketed past 2 million. More than half of those people live on the small island of Oahu and work in the sprawling city of Honolulu. Gridlock grinds our rush hours to a standstill, and everyone wonders why they didn't build a bigger freeway to begin with.

Foresight is invaluable when producing a vision. Take the time to plot your course carefully in the beginning, so you won't have to make major course corrections in the future. The time you spend on this will save you many sorrows in the years to come. If you are the new pastor of a church, a couple of silver trumpets will need to be hammered out based on your gifts and leadership style. You may use the same materials, same purpose and same assignment as the church used before, but hammer them out again until they blow clearly for you!

CUSTOM TRUMPETS ONLY, PLEASE!

The harder the conflict, the more glorious the triumph. What we obtain too cheap, we esteem too lightly; 'tis dearness only that gives everything its value. — Thomas Paine, *The American Crisis*

There will be trumpets for sale everywhere, trumpets that have been forged and hammered out by others. They will be for sale and readily available in every city, at most conferences, through the magazines and by mail order, but don't buy them! You can get trumpets from Chicago, Los Angeles, Korea, Toronto, Brownsville or even Hawaii. But don't do it. Hammer yours out for yourself! Sure it will take some time and effort, but it's well worth it! Only then will it blow clearly.

So what should we take back from others' ministries?

Take back hammering techniques. Learn principles and new perspectives, but don't buy ready-made trumpets. The reason they work so well in their own specific communities is that the leaders have taken the time to hammer them out for themselves. Each of us must do the same! Only you can know the needs and discern the distinct call God has for your life, for your ministry and, if you're a pastor, for your church. No one else will know your ministry the way you do. And when you take the time to hammer it out, you will find a depth of understanding and a quality that could never have been attained any other way. You'll begin to blow a clarion sound that will help others to catch the vision to do church as a team!

One of the churches we've had the privilege of partnering with is Willow Creek Community Church in South Barrington, Illinois. By partnering, what I really mean is that we attended many of their conferences and took copious notes on how Willow Creek became one of the biggest, most successful churches in America. How did they grow into a church with approximately 17,000 faithful attendees? We noticed the pursuit and practice of excellence in every aspect of their church, from the inside out. From the preaching of Senior Pastor Bill Hybels to the way they set up their website, every touch is personal, real, fresh and innovative. We've studied their books, the way they work with other churches and how they warmly receive new believers into the fold.

Now, although we have the highest esteem for the folks at Willow Creek, we would never dream of creating a cookie-cutter copy of their Chicago-area church in Hawaii. It would never work! Why? Because we have two very different constituencies, two very distinct congregations. What we did do, however, is apply some of their hammering techniques in the way we pounded out our own trumpet. Whereas Willow Creek has a food court filled with midwest cuisine like hot dogs, we have potlucks laden with the many ethnic dishes of Hawaii. We liked the warm way they received new believers, so we set up a Yes!

table outside our own services. We enjoyed their website design and adapted our own site to reflect a similar innovative realness to appeal to the people of Hawaii.

When you attend a conference, read a leadership book (even this book) or hear about the latest move of God in another church, I would encourage you to not superimpose that vision onto your own church. This is not to say that learning is not valuable, for a desire to continually learn is the mark of a visionary. However, I am saying that simplistic duplication is not valuable and, in fact, may hurt your organization.

Don't buy someone else's trumpet and attempt to play the same tune at your church. You'll only hit sour notes.

Learn hammering techniques; don't copy styles. Learn how they do what they do well, but don't buy their trumpet and attempt to play the same tune back home. Your people will have a unique style, as unique as the flavor of their foods and their brand of music. Honor your people by hammering out your own trumpet for your church.

TWO TRUMPETS ARE ETERNALLY BETTER THAN ONE

And when both are blown, all the congregation shall gather themselves to you at the doorway of the tent of meeting. Yet if only one is blown, then the leaders, the heads of the divisions of Israel, shall assemble before you. But when you blow an alarm, the camps that are pitched on the east side shall set out (Num. 10:3-5).

This Scripture reveals a couple of other interesting vision-building principles. First, God designated different trumpet blasts for different purposes. Second, Moses was to make for himself *two* trumpets. God designed it this way so that Moses had to recruit and train others from the very beginning. You see, Moses only had one set of lips, so someone had to be shadowing Moses and learning to lead as a team!

Our success as servant-leaders will depend in part on bringing others alongside us who know the vision, live the vision and help cast the vision. Moses didn't have forever on this side of eternity. He had to have a replacement, and God made provision for future leaders at the inception of the process. Even in our own lives and ministries, there's just too much to do for one person to do it all alone. Bring other servant-leaders alongside you, share the wealth of ministry that's available, and never, never go it alone! That's a surefire prescription for ministry suicide.

These trumpet principles show us that a critical part of authoring a clarion call is to hammer out your own trumpet. Remember, we should learn hammering techniques from one another, but never take another's trumpet as your own. The best sound will always come from a trumpet you've made for your own life or ministry. And be sure you hammer out two trumpets so that you venture into every endeavor as a team.

These biblical principles will help to set up the process for catching and then casting vision. Next, we must begin writing out our vision, and there are several guidelines to help you be the wordsmith of a great vision.

GUIDELINES FOR A GOD-GLORIFYING VISION

Every church needs a clear vision with certain qualities to ensure that the vision is indeed God-glorifying:

1. *The vision must be birthed and aligned with the Word of God.* God's Word is infallible; our desires or goals are not. Be sure that the Bible confirms your dreams and that there is never a conflict there. Is there a key verse or passage that embodies your vision? Ask God to reveal it to you. He will. "All Scripture is inspired by God and profitable for teaching, for reproof, for correction, for training in righteousness; that the man of God may be adequate, equipped for every good work" (2 Tim. 3:16,17).

2. *The vision must be consistent with the Great Commission for reaching the lost.* Every church should have at its core a passion for the lost. We can have goals for success, nurturing and discipleship, but if we are not bringing people to Christ, we have missed the point! "Go therefore and make disciples of all the nations, baptizing them in the name of the Father and the Son and the Holy Spirit, teaching them to observe all that I commanded you" (Matt. 28:19,20).

3. *The vision must be hammered out.* Your whole heart must be in the vision, and this is best done by ham-

mering out your own trumpet/vision for your life and your ministry. If your heart is not in it, if it is simply another program from another ministry, you will not pursue it aggressively. If God has indeed given you a vision, then He will give you the passion to fuel that vision and see it come to pass. He will also make available all the resources needed to see it through. "Make two silver trumpets for yourself; you shall make them of hammered work" (Num. 10:2).

4. *The vision must be clear, concise and easily understood by everyone.* Make sure the language in which you communicate the vision is clear, easily understood and to the point. If all are to catch the vision, they must first understand what it means, and everyone must catch the vision to guarantee complete success. "Then the LORD answered me and said, 'Record the vision and inscribe it on tablets, that the one who reads it may run'" (Hab. 2:2).

5. *The vision must guide every activity.* Vision cannot be a neat platitude or a nice saying in a booklet somewhere. It must be the compass that guides all your activities. Churches without a clear commission or statement of purpose are like ships without rudders. Make the vision plain and always visible as a reminder of God's call for the church. "If you know these things, you are blessed if you do them" (John 13:17).

The writer of Hebrews admonishes us to "run with endurance the race that is set before us" (Heb. 12:1). Each of us is accountable to run the race that God has set before us. Every church has a specific, unique assignment and direction, and we will stand accountable for the completion and fulfillment of that call. Not all churches are the same. Each has its own unique style, or thumbprint, and its vision must be processed and refined until everyone feels an ownership in it.

Remember this: People need a vision, but a vision needs people. You can have a vision, but if nobody buys into it, you don't have anything.

We must all have the commitment to jump into the things of the kingdom of God with reckless abandon and be wild for Him. We must have the passion to do whatever it takes. We must be like the disciples of Jesus and say, "We're gonna go for it! We've got one chance to serve Jesus before He comes, when we will go to heaven forever and never see a non-Christian for all of eternity. This is our only chance to do something to make a difference." When you catch that fire in your bosom, *then* things start to happen. When you catch a glimpse of eternity, you'll feel the flames of urgency licking at your heart and firing your vision, and you will truly understand that vision is vitally important to the survival of your church and your ministry.

HOW NEW HOPE DID IT

With the fire of a clear vision burning in our hearts, and with these principles and guidelines set in place, New Hope ventured into the process of developing our own vision. We understood the tremendous importance of a clear and compelling vision, but pounding out our vision was by no means easy. Nevertheless, it was well worth the time, heart and effort we poured into this foundation of our church.

We started with the first two steps, aligning our vision with the Word of God, especially the Great Commission:

Go therefore and make disciples of all the nations, baptizing them in the name of the Father and the Son and the Holy Spirit, teaching them to observe all that I commanded you; and lo, I am with you always, even to the end of the age (Matt. 28:19,20).

This is the heart of Jesus for the Church as well as for the lost. These were His final words He left to us, a charge to go into the world. This one statement is the starting point for all our assignments, and it is here that we at New Hope found our call.

We noticed that the Great Commission can be broken into four distinct stages. Each of these stages is one of New Hope's four "pillars" that support our church and make up the major ministry clusters within our church organization.

Stage One: EVANGELISM

The first word of Matthew 28:19 tells us to "go." Jesus calls us to take the initiative and reach out. This means action! We call this stage *evangelism*. This is simply taking non-Christians and leading them to the Lord in such a way that they become Christians—transformed, forgiven, growing followers of Christ.

God never told the world to come to the Church; He told the Church to "go into all the world" (Mark 16:15). Therefore, each of us must take the initiative to reach out to our families and friends, inviting them to Jesus. And each church must take the initiative to take Jesus to the people!

Our Sunday morning services are designed to partner with our members in their attempts to win their friends and families to Christ. The ambiance, printed materials, music and message are all shaped to support this one goal.

Stage Two: EDIFICATION

The second stage is discipleship: "Make disciples of all the nations." We call this stage *edification*, which is building each individual in his or her faith. God never said to fill the churches with converts; He said to fill them with disciples.

Our goal at New Hope is to take a convert and build him or her into a disciple of the Lord. This is where our small groups and midweek services come in. We have a course and tape series called *Growing Deep, Growing Strong* that introduces each person to membership.

Stage Three: EQUIPPING

The third stage alludes to a further *equipping*, in which God encourages each of us to "observe all I have commanded you." Herein lies the beginning of fruitfulness and life transformation. This is putting into practice what we understand. It is not just in the knowing but in the *doing* that we are blessed. Jesus tells us, "If you know these things, *you are blessed if you do them*" (John 13:17, emphasis added).

The New Hope DESIGN course and Doing Church as a Team conferences play a large part in this stage. Equipping people by helping them discover, develop and deploy their gifts helps them to grow. Each person is encouraged to put his or her gifts into action so that God's promise for their lives will be fulfilled, even as they realize the fullness of their faith.

Stage Four: EXTENSION

Finally, Jesus calls us to take courage in reaching out to others. The Lord assures us that He will accompany us: "And lo, I am with you even until the end of the age." We call this stage *extension*, in which we close the loop, with all of us reaching out and inviting someone else, even as we were invited!

Interestingly, these four stages—evangelism, edification, equipping and extension—build on one another. They flow naturally, marking each phase of the maturing process of every Christian from salvation to disciple to fruitful leader who goes out and reaches others for Christ. This is the beauty of God's master plan.

From these four stages, inspired by the Great Commission, was birthed the mission statement of New Hope Christian Fellowship:

> The purpose of New Hope is to present the Gospel of Jesus Christ in such a way that turns non-Christians into converts (EVANGELISM), converts into disciples (EDIFI-CATION) and disciples into mature, fruitful leaders (EQUIPPING), who will in turn go into the world and reach others for Christ (EXTENSION).

This mission guides everything we do. It is the trumpet of New Hope that we use to summon people to God's purposes. It must be blown consistently and clearly in order for us to paddle together as a team, each of us heading in the same direction with the same heart and same goals.

What happens when people lack a common vision? Simply this: Even though you are together, you have no idea where it is you are going. Always remember, people without a vision perish (see Prov. 29:18, *KJV*). No amount of unity on the part of the people will compensate for a lack of vision on the leader's part. Without a clear and compelling vision, all will fall and the ministry will have gone to waste. It will be fruitless because the people won't know where it is that God is leading them. They won't know what purpose they are meant to fulfill. "For if the bugle produces an indistinct sound, who will prepare himself for battle?" (1 Cor. 14:8).

MAKE IT A LASTING VISION

Your church must find its own course, its own race and its own calling. Only then will you be able to confidently set your compasses and navigate the ocean of decisions that you will encounter.

In scientific research, when a basic premise is incorrect, subsequent conclusions will also be wrong. This holds true for churches, too. If our premise, our purpose or our values are unsure, then every conclusion thereafter will follow suit. Our confidence in our calling will be shaky at best. A sure foundation is one of compelling vision, and that starts with a dream.

There's a dream springing up in the hearts of God's churches today. It's a dream with an edge to it, a vision. And that vision is becoming a rallying banner, uniting the hearts of God's people again.

This dream is nothing new. It's as old as the Bible itself. In fact, you'll find this dream sheathed within the fine pages of the

Word, which commands us to go forth and make disciples of all the nations as one Body, the Body of Christ.

We are many churches, internationally identified but in Christ unified. Through our common identity as the Body of Christ, we express the fullness of who Jesus is to our world. That's what the Church is designed to do. That's His great plan for all of us. That's how we become the fulfillment of God's greatness, for together we can obey God more fully than any one of us could alone.

That's His dream for us, and that dream has become the vision for His Church, expressed here simply as doing church as a team. And this vision is turning the hearts of churches across the land, across great bodies of water and across surging oceans, to unite in His cause and His heart. And what a dream it is! There is none better!

Set your compass according to God's instructions. Hammer out your purpose and assignment until that certain trumpet blows absolutely clear. Then with confidence, you'll be able to run the race. And as you run your race triumphantly, you'll find all around you not only a cloud of witnesses cheering you from the heavenlies but also a throng of like-hearted saints running right alongside you.

Notes

1. Lewis Carroll, *Alice's Adventures in Wonderland,* in Martin Gardner, *The Annotated Alice* (New York: New American Library, 1960), p. 88.
2. Stephen R. Covey, *The Seven Habits of Highly Effective People* (New York: Simon and Schuster, 1989), pp. 99, 100. Although Covey may have a different doctrine from ours, still we can learn from him. Receiving principles from his writing does not mean that you espouse his theology. It simply means that you are a seeker of truth, regardless of where the truth is found.

CHAPTER SEVEN STUDY GUIDE

1. What is your church's mission statement? Can you write it from memory? Where is this mission statement displayed?

2. If you've been to a conference lately, what are some hammering techniques you have learned? Why are these better than buying ready-made trumpets?

3. If you are a ministry leader in your church, write a mission statement for your ministry, making sure that it is in line with your church's overarching mission statement.

4. What is your dream? What is the God-given, God-designed dream He has planted in your heart? If you had no obstacles whatsoever, what would you do? Why aren't you doing that now? How can you begin to move in that direction?

5. If you strongly disagree with and cannot subscribe to your church's mission statement, what should you do?

CHAPTER EIGHT

ALIGNMENT: THE POWER OF MOVING TOGETHER

Then the LORD answered me and said, "Record the vision and inscribe it on tablets, that the one who reads it may run."

HABAKKUK 2:2

WHEN I WAS PASTORING IN THE SMALL TOWN OF HILO ON THE BIG ISLAND OF HAWAII, MY WIFE, ANNA, AND I DECIDED WE WOULD BECOME AN OFFICIAL AMERICAN FAMILY AND PURCHASE A MINI-VAN. SO WE WENT SHOPPING AND PICKED OUT THE PERFECT ONE, THE ONE MY LOVELY WIFE LIKED. WE PROUDLY DROVE HOME IN OUR NEW MINIVAN, AND ALL WAS WELL—OR SO WE THOUGHT.

Within a few weeks, as my wife drove around town, she began to notice a problem with the handling of our new vehicle. She astutely diagnosed the mechanical malfunction and announced, "It's driving a little funny." So I hopped in to give it a whirl, certain that the problem couldn't be anything major. Sure enough, the minivan was veering to one side of the road, and I had to strain on the wheel to steer it back to the center. Any which way I turned, the vehicle pulled strongly to the right—so much so that I had to drive crooked to go straight!

So I took the car to a mechanic friend of mine. He asked what was wrong, and I said, "It's driving a little funny." He nodded understandingly, the wise sage of all things mechanical and technical. He looked under the hood, and then he hoisted the minivan up on a lift and inspected the underside. Finally he said, "It's your alignment. It's off. That's why the whole car pulls to one side when it should be going forward."

This master of the monkey wrench then taught me a lesson in alignment. He told me that any vehicle that was out of alignment would not function to its potential. The wheels wouldn't run straight unless they were all aligned straight. "When one has alignment," I can still hear my teacher intone reverently, "one achieves unity. And when one achieves unity, all is well."

A LARGE LESSON FROM THE LITTLE LOCUST

Consider the locust. Scripture says, "The locusts have no king, yet all of them go out in ranks" (Prov. 30:27). Despite their diminutive size and their status as pests, the locusts receive honorable mention in the Word of God. What is it about these small insects that merits such an honor?

Have you ever seen a swarm of locusts? Their movement is uncanny. They appear as a dark, writhing cloud, moving steadily and posing a serious threat to the livelihood of agriculturists. Given the advantages of modern technology, farmers are still largely helpless to prevent locusts from damaging their crops. Yes, locusts are among the smallest of creatures, but they become a mighty force when they move en masse. That's the power of moving together—the power of alignment.

DEFINING ALIGNMENT

The strength of any vision lies in alignment—that is, vision that is caught and shared by every person involved. A common vision is the product of every person living a life of character and hearing the same call—a shared pictured of a preferred, God-designed future. Everyone pulling together for the cause is one of the most powerful concepts in building teams.

But vision means little without alignment. You can have the most visionary ideals, but without alignment you will not be able to achieve them. If everyone in your church doesn't catch a common vision, success will remain beyond your reach. You need to keep it together with each other in order to arrive at a common goal.

If there's one thing worse than a church without vision, it's a church with many visions! In this kind of congregation, everyone lobbies for his or her own personal agenda, and the church ends up becoming a political assembly—not a single body, but a chaotic gathering of conflicted individuals, each one pulling for his or her own viewpoint. With too many visions, a church will sow the seeds of dissension at its very inception, and failure is inevitable. An old Greek proverb says "If you pursue two hares, both will escape you."

Without alignment, disharmony and disunity will prevail. The apostle Paul wrote the church at Philippi, "Make my joy complete by being of the same mind, maintaining the same love, united in spirit, intent on one purpose" (Phil. 2:2). Here Paul speaks about the joy of everyone in a group possessing the same heart and passion. He knew that there is nothing more beautiful than a congregation in which everyone marches from the same starting point, with the same heart, in the same direction and with the same cadence. This produces a joyous song with rhythm and harmony!

Alignment can help build an unstoppable movement able to overcome every obstacle, move every mountain and bridge every impasse. When everyone is in alignment, every daily activity contributes in a more meaningful way to the overall vision of the church.

RECORDING THE VISION

One of the first steps in building alignment is to let the people know where they are supposed to be headed! Alignment begins when your direction is commonly understood and echoed in the heart of every member.

My responsibility as a servant-leader is to shepherd God's people well by setting forth a mission statement, or statement of purpose, for the people He has me leading. I must communicate the vision in order for the people involved to catch it!

Each person has been called to run the race to win (see Heb. 12:1,2), but it is first the leader's call to set the vision clearly before the people so that they may run well. In his short but powerful Old Testament book, the prophet Habakkuk gives us this vital principle for building alignment:

> Then the LORD answered me and said, "Record the vision and inscribe it on tablets, *that the one who reads it may run.* For the vision is yet for the appointed time; it hastens toward the goal, and it will not fail. Though it tarries, wait for it; for it will certainly come, it will not delay" (Hab. 2:2,3, emphasis added).

God tells leaders to set a statement of purpose clearly before the people so that they may run in such a way that they will win. Knowing the vision and presenting it clearly are absolutely crucial to the success of any church or ministry.

At New Hope Christian Fellowship we continually communicate our mission statement to the whole church. We explain our vision and disseminate it in as many different ways as we can—from the pulpit, in our newsletter and weekly bulletins and in most of our flyers. We even post it in the reception area of our offices so that anyone who walks in, whether visitor or member, can read it and know what we're doing as a ministry. When we can all see the vision (the assignment of this church), we can all run together.

Even though we may have heard it many times before, we remind ourselves of the common vision so that we may stay in tune with each other and with our original purpose. That's a lesson we can take from the locusts. Though they have no king, they go out in ranks because they are single-minded in their purpose. Although we *do* have a King, we must be sure to check back in regularly to know fully His mission for us, so we can go out in ranks with a common call on our hearts.

God has called us to be a people of vision, with every single one of us pulling together in rhythm. Everyone has a paddle, so they have a part. In order for our canoe to arrive successfully at its destination, the people need to row together. We all must stroke together and not just stroke at our own pace. This takes character, to not overwhelm the weaker ones in the canoe or stray from the team effort by insisting on moving at our own pace. Paddling together propels us forward and results in progress.

New churches often split after a year or two because their leaders don't understand these principles. God placed them in the Scriptures so that every leader will have them deep within his or her heart. If you are a leader, set these principles firmly in your heart.

Take God's vision and write it down clearly, and teach your people to have a common vision. Everyone will have to have a common vision with the same heart. If they can't submit to that kind of vision, then that is not the place or ministry where they are supposed to be. You must have unity among the brethren. When you have unity within your ministry, your people will go forth in ranks. And like the locusts, who have no king but go out in ranks, the people who have caught the vision of your ministry will not need a leader constantly supervising them. You can release them to run!

ARROWS POINTING IN THE SAME DIRECTION

What does alignment look like? If we were to draw a picture of alignment, it should not be cloudy (though that seems to work for the locusts). Instead, let's represent each member or ministry of the congregation as an arrow to show that each of us has his or her own direction. If we are all in agreement with the overall mission of the church, then all of our arrows will be pointing in the same direction. When we're not in alignment, however, then we look like a mess of pixie sticks scattered on the ground.

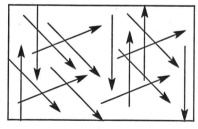 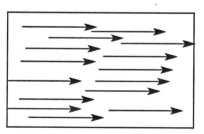

Church without alignment   **Church with alignment**

Which of these represents the flow of your ministry?

Whatever your situation, it's never too late to make adjustments and repair your alignment. The fact is that even if we are generally in alignment, we can only stay in alignment if we are making frequent course corrections—adjustments to the way we do church. Like automobile wheels reacting to bumps and curves in the road, we all have a natural tendency to shift during transit. So just as we do when we drive our cars, we must make constant minor course corrections or risk straying from the road and missing our goal.

One way to do this is by using frequent checkpoints along the way.

CONSTANTLY EVALUATING FOR SUCCESS

Just as we have many organs in our physical bodies, there will be many ministries in any healthy church—ministries for youth, men, women, small groups and children, to name a few. When there is proper alignment, these ministries will directly fulfill the church's overarching vision. They will constantly check to make sure their arrows (the direction of their ministry) are pointing in the same direction as the mission of the church. To do that, each ministry must continually review its strategy for fulfilling that general vision.

Each ministry must constantly evaluate itself, asking the following questions:

- Is our ministry producing disciples and mature leaders who are integrated into the context of the church? Or is the ministry an island unto itself with independent goals?

- In what way do we share vision with volunteers and staff? Is this method effective?
- How can we actively encourage alignment within our church? Our ministry?
- How do we regain alignment? Are there any course corrections we need to make within our ministry or church?

When each individual ministry and every individual member is pulling together in the same direction, then you begin doing church as a team. There's a synergy in this combined effort that far exceeds the strength of a single person or small group of individuals trying to do it alone. Two people doing the same task together will produce much more than twice the effort of just one. Three or more people doing church together increases synergy exponentially. And not only are physical energy and wisdom doubled, but when doing church as a team, we also gain anointing. Jesus promised, "Where two or three have gathered together in My name, there I am in their midst" (Matt. 18:20).

Make sure to keep that synergy and anointing by constantly reevaluating yourself, your ministry and your church. Ask yourself those key questions and make sure you're still on track. If you're not, no problem! Make any necessary corrections and no matter what, keep going!

DEFINING VALUES

The first phase of successful alignment is to constantly evaluate your ministry. The second practical phase of alignment is to identify your ministry's core values. A church's core values give each person a point of reference that acts like the North Star, providing your people with a sense of direction and cohesion in the ministry.

Values are like windows through which decisions are viewed. When confronted with a certain choice, we will tend to make the choice that is consistent with our values. Common values give everyone the same starting point and the same perspective. When people in the church are making decisions that are consistent with the core values, you achieve a wonderful synergy and a culture of balance and truth.

When a church's values are understood and echoed in the heart of every member, you have alignment.

Values can also be likened to a homing device, an internal guidance mechanism that keeps you on course. Values help you to make in-flight corrections to your attitudes, motives, activities and emphases. Each of us needs to make many in-flight corrections along the way, but if we have not clearly defined our core values, we won't know when or how to make course corrections! When a church's values are understood and echoed in the heart of every member, you have alignment.

Some years ago, I took a week of golf lessons. My instructor's goal was to teach me what the basic swing was to feel like and how the ball was to fly if I hit it correctly. The whole week was geared toward that single goal. Without a knowledge of the basic swing and what the flight of the ball should look like when hit correctly, I would have no point of reference for improving my swing in the future; even if I happened to hit a great shot, I wouldn't know what I had done to create such a shot, and I wouldn't be able to repeat it if I tried! Conversely, should I hit a terrible shot, I would have no idea why it went bad or how to correct it.

That's just like the Church sometimes, isn't it? We often just swing away, never really knowing why sometimes we hit the mark and why we miss it so badly at others. We may chalk the results up to a blessing or an attack, depending on the outcome, when really it has more to do with us not knowing our point of reference.

Knowing our core values is like knowing the basic golf swing—it sets a baseline that will guide us in knowing when we're hitting it and when we're missing it. That way we'll know which opportunities we get to say yes to and which ones we get to say no to. Commonly understood values help us to set our sights on the vision and increase our chances of achieving and maintaining alignment.

WRESTLING WITH A VISION FOR VALUES

We are responsible to catch our vision and values from the Lord and wrestle with them until we can articulate them clearly to others. This does not come easily. Sometimes the Lord will reveal it all in a moment, but this is not usually the case. Oftentimes, we are like Jacob, who wrestled all night until he saw daylight (see Gen. 32:24). Most leaders find that they must wrestle with their vision until the values become clear. This process may be heart- and soul-wrenching, but there are no shortcuts on this one.

At New Hope our declaration of nine core values grew out of a host of discussions about what it was we valued. I talked with dozens of leaders, received input from as many members as I could and tested the list over and over again by seeking further feedback, knowing that identifying these values would help us to clarify what is truly important and where we should be focusing our energies and resources.

Inspired by what I saw in Jesus, I also made a point to get alone and pray during this process. I went on a spiritual retreat to hear from the Lord about His will for our church. My retreats usually consist of getting away for two or three days to a neighboring island, where I hole myself up in a hotel to pray. It's during these times that I am best able to hear direction for my life and direction for the church.

I also went on retreat with our church's administrator (who is a dear friend to me), and our management team also congregated to help formulate the vision and core values of the church.

This wrestling exacted from us prayer and fasting, in-depth discussions and seeking the Lord's face for our church. But when it was done, the daylight streamed in and we had nine core values that made up the future reference point for every activity, every service and every member of New Hope.

NEW HOPE'S NINE CORE VALUES

At New Hope our values are a metronome that keeps us all paddling with the same cadence. These nine core values are principles we hold tightly to. They flavor every activity, and they balance every endeavor. Each member wholeheartedly subscribes to each one. In doing so, we can all have "the same love, united in spirit, intent on one purpose" (Phil. 2:2).

1. We believe that every person, Christian and non-Christian alike, is valuable to God and to His kingdom.
Because people are eternally valuable to God, they are valuable to us as well. Responsible evangelism will always be our cause, and ongoing discipleship will always be the core of the ministry (see Matt. 18:14; Matt. 25:45; 2 Pet. 3:9).

People are precious. They rank very high on God's ledger, and if we are going to be a people after God's own heart, they had better rank pretty high on ours as well! We must love them with His love and care for them with His compassion. People are eternal, and their eternal welfare is much more important than their present behavior. Looking past who they are and seeing them for what they can be will always open new doorways to ministry and miracles.

This doesn't mean we become people pleasers. We are here to please an audience of One! Loving people means that we are committed to God's very best for their lives. If God's best means overlooking a fault or indiscretion, then we will comply. If God's best is to confront, then we will confront with love.

Even in the case of evangelism, we must be sensitive to a person's readiness to receive the gospel. We, as Christians, can be insensitive to people; in our zeal to convert them, we can do more damage than good. Responsible evangelism and ongoing discipleship are central to our calling.

2. We believe that doing church as a team is God's design for effective ministry.

Spirit-empowered service with the willing-hearted involvement of every person is vital to God's plan being accomplished (see Ps. 133:1; Eccles. 4:9-12; Eph. 4:11-16; 1 Pet. 2:4-9).

The day of the Lone Ranger is over. If we are going to be effective in this new century, everyone in the Church must realize his or her importance to God's plan. We are called the Body of Christ, not the collection of body parts of Christ. Everyone has a place, a function and a purpose; but we've got to learn to work together. There's just no substitute! And the more people take ownership of the ministry, the stronger a church becomes.

3. We believe that a simple presentation of Jesus Christ in creative ways will impact and transform lives.

Relating to our culture through redeeming the arts while remaining true to the Scriptures is a balance we will always keep. This allows us to present the gospel in such a way that reaches the heart (see Acts 17:22-24; 1 Cor. 9:22,23).

People aren't tired of the gospel; they're tired of tired presentations of the gospel. The gospel is the power of God to transform lives! It isn't boring; it is powerful! When the gospel is preached, the Holy Spirit takes down-and-out drug addicts and turns them into saints. He takes broken marriages and restores them. He takes hopeless lives and breathes new beginnings into them. But remember this one thing: The Holy Spirit's responsibility is to assure that the message is true, not necessarily interesting. That's *our* responsibility!

So while remaining true to the Scriptures, we work through creative ways to present the claims of Christ. We will use anything we can to help people understand just how wonderful and precious the Word of God is. Hebrews tells us that the Word is "living and active" (Heb. 4:12), so if we can plant it deep in a person's soul, the Lord will do the rest! But first, we must use good soil so that the seed can take root!

I remember when this fact first struck me. I was reading Matthew 13, the parable of the sower and the seed. Jesus describes the varying soils in which seed is sown, and He likens them to the varying responses of the human heart. Only once does the devil enter the story. And how does the devil find entry?

> When anyone hears the word of the kingdom, *and does not understand it,* the evil one comes and snatches away what has been sown in his heart (Matt. 13:19, emphasis added).

When someone doesn't understand the Word that has been sown in his or her heart, the devil takes the opportunity to snatch it away. That hit me like a ton of bricks! I thought to myself, *If I am the preacher and I am sowing the Word, then I must do my best to make sure each listener understands. Now what they do with it after that is up to them, but I must communicate in such a way that the truth impacts their hearts. I've just got to be sure they understand it!*

For weeks and months I thought about this. I knew the good news needed to be made simple to understand, creative in presentation and accurate in content. I had to take the cookies off the top shelf and put them on the lower shelf, so everyone could grasp them. I just *had* to help people understand the gospel!

If multimedia helps, then I will use it. If a dance, a mime, a song or a sketch will better present the gospel so that people can better understand it, then I will redeem that method for the gospel's sake! If by tap dancing I could help people's eyes see the truths of the Bible, then I would learn to tap dance!

We will not use multimedia or the performing arts just because we want to be part of the latest trend or because other churches are doing so. We use the arts because we can help people to better understand the Word! We will never compromise the truths or accuracy of the Bible for an art form. God's Word never changes, but cultures do. Therefore, we will anchor ourselves to His ageless truths but gear the style with which we present those truths to the times we are living in.

4. We believe every member should commit to a lifestyle of consistent spiritual growth with honest accountability.
A genuine love for God is always a first priority (see Mark 12:30). Every Christian should yearn for continual spiritual growth. Therefore, discipleship through small groups, accountability and open honesty are critical to maturing in our faith (see Prov. 27:17; Mark 12:31; Acts 2:44-47; 1 Tim. 4:7,8; 1 Pet. 2:2).

There are two kinds of Christians in the world today: One knows what to do, and the other does what he or she knows. Our ranks are crowded with the first, and this is a serious problem. The symptoms are easily recognizable. Many of us know all there is to know about joy, but there's no joy in our families. We know all there is to know about forgiveness, but we just can't seem to forgive our spouses or parents.

One of the best ways to bridge this discrepancy is through small groups. In these huddles of friends, we can support one another, graciously remind one another of what we believe and hold each other accountable. All pretenses are minimized when you get up close and personal!

5. We believe that every member is a minister who has been given gifts to be discovered, developed and deployed.
We are a gift-based, volunteer-driven church. Each believer will find his greatest joy and fulfillment when serving in his gifts and passion. Every believer is created for ministry, gifted for ministry, authorized for ministry and needed for ministry (see Mark 10:45; Rom. 12; 1 Cor. 12:14-20; Eph. 2:10).

No one is unimportant! I continually remind our members that everyone is a 10 somewhere. God has deposited within each of us one or more gifts through which we can make an eternal contribution. As each person finds his or her place and begins serving through his or her gifts, the church will run together with maximum effectiveness and minimum weariness.

6. We believe that God is worthy of our very best. Therefore, a growing spirit of excellence should permeate every activity.
Not perfection, but excellence with consistent evaluation and a willingness to improve for the sake of the kingdom of God are distinctive of growing ministries (see Ps. 78:72; Eccles. 10:10; Dan. 5:12; Col. 3:17).

There is no greater vision, no more compelling invitation than to serve the King of kings! He is indeed worthy of our very best.

We serve an excellent God, and because we are created in His image, we can be an excellent people. Excellence can only truly be achieved in our actions when it first appears in the heart behind our actions.

7. We believe that genuine love and caring relationships are key to the life of every endeavor.
Refusing to give audience to a spirit of complaining, we will instead be

courageous in solving every problem in a way that honors God and builds biblical character. We value healthy relationships and protect the unity of the Spirit in our church (see Rom. 16:17; 1 Cor. 13:8; Eph. 4:3; Jas. 1:2,3; 1 Pet. 5:8,9).

One element common to all growing churches is problems. It's unfortunate but true that problems come with the territory. Growing pains such as crowded parking, long lines and short-handed classrooms will continue to be common to expanding twenty-first-century ministries. We have decided, however, that complaining will not be an option at New Hope. We must face and confront every problem head-on and in a timely fashion. This is to be done in such a way that will honor the Lord and result in the building of biblical character.

8. We believe that the most effective evangelism happens through people inviting people.

We believe that a life will reach a life. Each believer develops genuine relationships with friends and family and extends an invitation to them. Evangelism gets to be a normal, natural lifestyle of winning others to Christ, one by one (see Prov. 11:30; John 1:43-45, 4:28-30).

The greatest evangelist is not Billy Graham, D. L. Moody or the pastor of some megachurch. The most effective evangelists are the individuals who make up the Church. Every Christian has unchurched loved ones—friends or family members in need of the saving grace of Jesus Christ. Through these genuine relationships, a verbal witness is given or an invitation extended, and often an unchurched person becomes willing to investigate the claims of Christianity.

Sue Ann is a New Hope member who was on fire with the excitement of a new believer. We were at a Rotary convention where I saw her seated at a table, conversing with an elderly Japanese gentleman. Although she was much younger, they seemed to be old friends. I made my way over to greet her, and she introduced me to Mr. Hatada. And without hesitating on our account, Sue Ann launched into one of the finest evangelical campaigns I have ever witnessed.

"Mr. Hatada, do you go to church?"

"No," he replied. "I am a Buddhist."

"Then you *must* come to our church!"

I chuckled under my breath at Sue Ann's somewhat disconnected reply. Mr. Hatada, presuming she had misunderstood him, repeated his answer.

"No," he protested. "You see, I'm a Buddhist."

"That's okay!" she said optimistically. "You just *have* to come to our church! Even just once! Just come. You'll love it! You won't be the same."

"Well, I have my own religion," he said. "It's giving money to charitable organizations like the Boy Scouts and the United Way."

"That's great," Sue Ann shot back, "but you just *have* to come to our church!"

"But I golf on Sundays," Mr. Hatada finally admitted.

"That's fine, but you *must* come to our church!"

By this time, I was quite intrigued with her unique method of evangelism. For 20 minutes she gave the same reply to every one of his arguments. Whatever reason he gave for his unwillingness or inability to accept her invitation, Sue Ann remained gracious but unwavering: "That's fine, Mr. Hatada, but you just *have* to come to our church!"

He could have said, "No, you see I'm an alien from Alpha Centauri," and her reply would have remained the same: "That's fine, but you just have to come to our church. Come just once, and you'll never be the same!" I remember chuckling to myself and thinking, *You can't teach this kind of evangelism in Bible college. This comes straight from the heart!*

You see, when people are excited about what God is doing in their church, evangelism becomes a natural by-product! Our eighth core value helps us keep this well in mind. We know without a doubt that no ministry, program or event will be as effective in winning souls to Christ as a real live person is in reaching another person one-one-one.

This is because the best form of evangelism is *Emmanuelism*, people recognizing that God is with us. And that can happen in gatherings of two and three family members, coworkers or friends—people who care enough to communicate Christ to the people in their lives. This value captures the heart of our church family and has truly become an important core value.

9. We believe in identifying and training emerging leaders who are fully committed to Christ and who will reach their generation with the gospel.
God is raising up men and women who will take the baton of godly character, authentic faith and servant-hearted leadership into the next generation (see Ps. 78:6,7; 1 Tim. 3:1; 2 Tim. 2:2; Titus 1:5-9).

This core value is a constant reminder to give life away, to increase the base of leadership and to unselfishly live to make others successful. The ultimate test of a successful leader is not necessarily found in what he does but, rather, in what others are doing as a result of what he has done.

THE HEART AND PASSION OF NEW HOPE

These core values, in tandem with our church's mission statement, make up the heart and passion of New Hope Christian Fellowship. They are the premise upon which we base all that we do. It is our goal for members to own these values so much that it permeates everything they do and say.

The heart and passion of New Hope are the very things that make us unique and are second in importance only to Jesus, for they compose the personality our church embodies—the very essence of our being. Without our heart and passion, we would be a set of dry doctrines at best. With them, we have become a warm-hearted ministry, alive with God's love and passionate for His purposes.

If we were to alter our heart or passion in any way, we would be an altogether different church, for our expressed core values and mission establish our culture in every ministry and project.

BUILDING A COMMON CULTURE

As alignment falls into place and those involved in the ministry catch the heart of the vision and core values, your church will begin to develop a common culture. Your overarching mission statement will direct your course and influence the thinking, actions and beliefs of every member to the point that everyone is believing, doing and saying the same things.

Let's say that you were hired by a large supermarket to stock the shelves. So you arrive at the specified time on your first day, and you are told to stock the canned goods along with a few other workers. After a moment or two, you strike up a conversation: "How long you been working here?" you ask a fellow worker.

"About a year," he replies.

"I just hired on yesterday," you say. "I've never met the owner. What is it like to work here?"

Your coworker gruffly says, "Just do your job and you won't have any problems. Keep your nose clean, your mouth shut and your eyes open. Pick up your paycheck and stay out of the customers' way. Got it?"

And so your first day begins. You now have an impression of the whole company, even before you meet the owner. Your fellow worker has established something of the corporate culture for you. By lunchtime, you're ready to check the classified ads for another job opportunity.

Let's try it again. It's your first day on the job and you strike up the same conversation with a coworker—except this time things go a bit differently.

"How long you been working here?" you ask.

"About a year," he replies.

"I just hired on yesterday. I've never met the owner. What kind of place is this to work at?"

Your coworker turns to you, smiles and says, "It's wonderful! I mean, the people here are like family to me. The owner is caring and interested in everyone. You'll absolutely love it! It won't be long before you will feel like family, too. Here, take a moment and let me introduce you to the other stock clerks."

And off you go with a wholly different feeling. Although you've never met the owner, you love the place! You have a feeling that you're going to enjoy working here.

You see, everyone in a church has a ministry of sharing their culture with visitors and new members. How do church members, staff and volunteers know what their culture is? Typically they learn it through the sermons, classes, teachings, personal relationships and small groups, all of which express the church's core values.

Culture can be defined as the way a church's members interact socially with one another, but basically, a culture is defined by its values. Whatever you hold dear in your heart will influence the actions of your hands. The Bible says, "Watch over your heart with all diligence, for *from it flow the springs of life*" (Prov. 4:23, emphasis added). Whatever is dear to the people's hearts is what will flow through who they are and will spring to life.

For example, a particular church might place a high value on evangelism, so the members focus on saving souls. Socially, they value interaction centered around food and fellowship, so they love to hold potlucks and find ways to have fun with one another. Intellectually, they may lean more on New Testament thought than on the Old Testament.

What happens is that this particular church gears its weekend services to be highly seeker-friendly. The music, drama and message are modern, alive and relevant to what people are going through every day. The church is not only seeker-friendly on the inside but on the outside as well: To encourage fellowship and fun, the members have set up huge food and ministry tents in their courtyard. This all stems from the church's culture, the values they hold dear.

A culture, then, is the sum of a church's parts—its core values in action. It's in what they teach, in the way they interact and in what they believe. The culture stems from the core values, which are inspired by a common vision.

FINISHING WELL

About 25 years ago, an Olympic marathon went down in the annals of sports history, not for its greatness, but for its tragic ending. The race started with the highest of hopes, each nation represented proudly by its best male runner, each athlete representing years of superhuman training, extreme endurance and thousands of hours of running. These men were in their prime, the elite of an entire nation—literally the best of the best.

The starting gun fired, launching each man into a surge of beatific athleticism. Watching their explosive sprint out of the blocks, you would never guess this was to be an extended marathon. Yet as the runners settled into their rhythmic pacing, the crowd settled in also, knowing even the fastest man would be about two hours before returning to the finish. The marathon would conclude back where it started, in front of the grandstands full of spectators. In the meantime, they ran their course outside the stadium, while other field events took place inside.

Two hours and four minutes later the first runner was sighted making his return, and the track was cleared. The leader was way ahead of everybody else, and the crowd cheered, straining to see him in the darkness of the tunnel leading into the stadium. When he broke into the sunlight, the runner was clearly delirious with exhaustion. He stumbled but quickly got back up. The cheering stadium fell silent. It was as though he had lost his sense of direction. He didn't know which way to go. His eyes were glazed. He was obviously in a lot of pain but on he ran.

Then he stopped again, looked around in a daze and started running the other way! One of the coaches leaped from the stands to help him. "Get back," an Olympic official warned. "You can't touch him! If you touch him, that's it; he's disqualified. He'll be out of the race!" The coach stepped back, but the crowd began yelling directions to the runner. He still had a chance to win the gold and glory, because the other runners weren't even in sight yet. Despite the sheer volume of the stadium crowd yelling, he was too dazed to hear anything. He ran one way, looked around, ran the other way and finally fell down and just lay there.

The crowd was on its feet by then, urgently shouting, "Get up! Get up!" He struggled to stand and slowly stumbled to the finish, collapsing across the line. The crowd went crazy. Within minutes, the other runners entered the stadium and completed the race.

When the final accolades were handed out, however, the announcer shocked everyone by saying the fastest runner, the man who had beaten everyone else, was disqualified. The reason involved the fact that there were two finish lines: one line for sprints that were soon to be run and the other line, for the marathon. The "winner" ran to the wrong finish line and collapsed across it. Prior to the race, he had been informed and was well aware that the actual destination for the marathon runners was on the other end of the track; but because of his delirium, the runner forgot and finished at the wrong line. He had run superbly, apparently the best athlete that day, but he lost it all. Because he lost his sense of direction, he didn't even place.

Think how more tragic it would be if you ran hard your whole life but finished poorly because you didn't accomplish what God asked you to accomplish. You didn't run the race set before you, and though you ran hard, you finished somebody else's race. As you cross the finish line, you may think, *Wow, look at that! The crowd is going bananas!*

The Lord says, "But I asked you to run a different race. I equipped you to run a particular race."

You protest, "Yeah, but I ran this race, and everybody is so excited!"

In the end, though, the Lord is Judge; and only He can qualify or disqualify you, according to your obedience to His call for you. That's why Paul says, "I must consider everything else as nothing in order that I might finish well the race set before me" (see Acts 20:24).

Alignment is important to our finishing the race well. If you are a leader, make sure you catch God's vision for you and communicate it clearly to the people that they might also run the race to win. Create an environment for effective ministry by setting the church's sights toward a common vision and setting the church's heartbeat to a common culture through expressed values. You will find the people in your ministry sharing a vibrant heart and a passion that fuel every step and every breath of every endeavor.

And when you run the right race, headed in the right direction, you'll have a much better chance of finishing well!

CHAPTER EIGHT STUDY GUIDE

1. Write a definition of alignment. What does this mean for you and to your church?

2. What are some reasons for establishing core values early on in a ministry? What will these values help you to do?

3. What are your church's core values? If you haven't written them down yet, think about the values your church holds dear—as reflected in their social, moral and intellectual practices—and then begin to record them for your church.

4. How do you communicate your core values to the congregation? How often?

5. Can there be a difference between core values and culture? How does that happen? How can this affect alignment?

BUILDING TEAMS

*Our bodies have many parts, but the many parts make up only one
body when they are all put together. So it is with the "body" of Christ.*

1 CORINTHIANS 12:12, *TLB*

DOING CHURCH AS A TEAM IS A WHOLE NEW MIND-SET FOR OUR CHURCHES TODAY. BUT IF WE ARE GOING TO BE A CHURCH OF THE TWENTY-FIRST CENTURY, THERE'S JUST NO OTHER WAY! THE DAYS OF THE LONE RANGER ARE OVER. OFTEN IN THE BIBLE, GOD REFERS TO US AS THE BODY OF CHRIST. THE BETTER WE UNDERSTAND THIS METAPHOR, THE MORE WE WILL BE ABLE TO COOPERATE WITH GOD'S DESIGN FOR THE CHURCH.

The church is not an organization. It is more like an *organism* with living parts that must move and work together as a whole. An individual part cannot stand on its own. If I cut off my arm and planted it in dirt, that arm would not grow into a new body; it would die! So it is with the Body of Christ. Each of us has an individual assignment and role, but apart from the rest of the Body, we are useless. God created us that way. That is *His* design, not ours.

Have you ever noticed how each part of your physical body works in groups? For example, the hand works with five fingers, a palm, a wrist and forearm, with muscles, bones and tendons connecting them all together. The integration of all these elements working together gives your composite hand and forearm agility and coordination. You see, every part of your body works best as a team, with all of its parts serving in harmony and cooperation toward a common goal!

Have you ever watched a concert pianist moving his fingers in perfect synchronization, running arpeggios up and down the keys of a piano? Each sinew, each ligament, every finger, muscle and joint work together to create a symphony of notes blended together in beautiful harmony. No one finger could accomplish what the score called for. The wrist couldn't do it alone, and neither could the arm. But working together, each part fulfilling its role, they can fill a concert hall with magnificent music that enthralls an audience and sets their hearts soaring.

This is the Church—connected to "the Head, that is, Christ" (Eph. 4:15, *NIV*) and working together for the "common good" (1 Cor. 12:7)! Each of us is to be a living, functioning, serving member of the Body of Christ. God has gifted each of us with talents and abilities. He has divinely endowed us with all we need to serve His purposes, and we do this best in teams.

Building teams does not begin with a certain kind of technique; it begins with a certain kind of heart. This is an unselfish, authentic heart, desiring only God's best. Such a heart constantly asks, *How can I include others?* It anticipates the joy of sharing experiences, struggles and victories, realizing that, like the body, we work best in teams—the way God designed us to function.

THE BEGINNINGS OF FRACTAL TEAM BUILDING

I owe much of the understanding of this metaphor to a longtime friend, Loren Cunningham, the president and founder of Youth With A Mission. The first time I met him was in Hilo nearly two decades ago. Loren is a big man, standing over six feet tall. I remember the first time I shook his hand. Mine disappeared in his, and I was secretly glad to get it back. Well, his heart is as big as he is.

Last summer, Loren was visiting Hawaii. We were having lunch together in Waikiki on a balmy Sunday afternoon with my good friend Danny Lehman joining us. During the meal, I asked Loren if he wouldn't mind sharing some ideas he had garnered along the way on equipping God's people to reach the lost. That one question ignited three hours of brisk interchange and conversation. He shared with me a seed thought about *fractal patterns*, which he had heard Winkey Pratney discuss in one of his seminars. We sat and talked until it looked like the waiter was about to charge us double for loitering.

This process for building teams is by no means the only way. There are dozens of time-tested ways to build teams, and no one way is necessarily the best. Find one that works best for you and do it! The bottom line is this: You can't do it alone! You weren't designed to. So what you will read in these next few pages is the way we at New Hope have found that works well for us. We're still hammering it out, but it works splendidly with our style and makeup.

THE CHURCH: A LIVING ORGANISM

According to *Webster's Dictionary*, the word "fractal" means "any of various extremely irregular curves or shapes for which any suitably chosen part is similar in shape to a given larger or smaller part when magnified or reduced to the same size."[1]

Now if you're anything like me, you're just as much in the dark after reading the definition as you were before. Let me see if I can explain it as it pertains to doing church as a team.

Living organisms are, in some aspects, very similar to organizations, while in other ways they are very different. For instance, both require structure, direction, measurable objectives and leadership. On the other hand, an organism is a living entity with emotions, changes, natural growth and a susceptibility to diseases, accidents, predators and sicknesses.

The Church, or the Body of Christ, is a living organism. It may have organizational needs, but organization alone would cause it to be unhealthy. Like a silk plant, the Church could look fine on the outside but be lifeless on the inside. Silk plants often look wonderful from a distance, but up close, you can tell there's no life or fragrance to them.

Sometimes it seems easier to treat the Church as an organization because, like silk plants, once they've been arranged, the maintenance required is nil. They look good, but don't get too close! Recall with me the fig tree in the book of Mark: "And seeing at a distance a fig tree in leaf, He went to see if perhaps He would find anything on it; and when He came to it, He found nothing but leaves" (Mark 11:13). Jesus actually cursed the fig tree, and it withered up! The tree looked good from a distance, but up close there was no evidence of fruit.

THE REPEATING PATTERN

The fractal design for doing church as a team is more akin to living organisms than anything I have seen so far. Despite the unwieldy origins of the name, it's a simple concept that works. Simply put, it's a structure that repeats itself over and over again.

Take the fern, for example. Here in Hawaii, these plants grow everywhere. If you look at the fern plant in its entirety, you will see one major stem with smaller branches extending from it on either side. Now take a closer look at one of the branches. You will see the same structure duplicated with a major stem and smaller leaves extending. If your eyesight is good, observe closely one of the individual leaves. You will see that very same structure duplicated again with a major vein running down the middle of the leaf with several more extending from it. If you had a microscope, you could see that structure duplicated again and again.

Our bodies have a similar fractal design. Physically, we see one major unit called the human body with limbs extending. Take one of the limbs and you'll see within it a major artery with several branching off it. Then take one of the secondary arteries and you will see again several more branching off until every area of the body is reached for circulation and health.

Doing church as a team uses this fractal design—a very simple, repeating pattern that is found in most organisms. Each unit has similar patterns and similar purposes.

For the sake of simplicity, we build our teams in groupings of five (or, if working with couples, groupings of ten). The reason for this is that it seems to work best for providing appropriate spans of care.

DOWNWARD GROWTH

Here's how it works. Let's say I am asked to help with the church's children's ministry. My passion is to work with kids, and I have some teaching gifts and organizational skills. I would love to work with the children, so I say yes.

In doing church as a team, my first move is not to jump in and start working with the children. Instead, my first step is to build a team of four leaders with whom I will serve. When I choose the four, we have a team totaling five people with similar passions and supportive gifts.

Now let's say that the age range covered by our children's ministry will be from newborns through fourth graders. So we form our teams which are (1) nursery and toddlers, (2) prekindergarten and kindergarten, (3) first and second grade and (4) third and fourth grade. The following graph illustrates this:

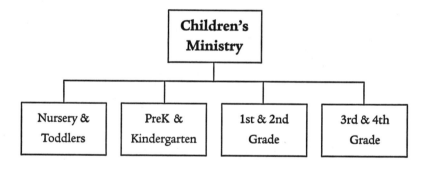

Using the fractal design, I find a person who loves babies. When this nursery and toddler leader agrees to be part of the children's ministry team, he or she does *not* immediately jump in and start working with the babies. Instead, duplicating the pattern of what was just done, the nursery leader builds a team of four other leaders with similar passions and supporting gifts. So another team is built to serve the nursery and toddlers.

Here's an example of how it might look when the nursery and toddler leader builds a team:

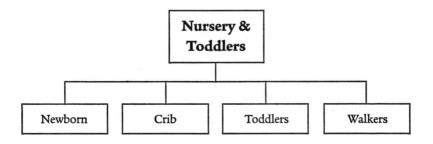

Each of the other leaders—prekindergarten and kindergarten, first and second grade team and the third and fourth grade team—does exactly the same thing, duplicating the team-building process.

Then if you add all the teams up, with the four main leaders each serving with four on their individual teams, the leadership of the children's ministry grows immediately to 21 people. And that's just going two deep. This pattern can be continued by duplicating building out to a third or even a fourth level. As large as the ministry grows, the teams simply grow deeper.

You see, with this pattern of ministry, growth is downward. That is to say that the larger the ministry grows, the deeper the levels of teams you build. For example, if the nursery and toddler team has its four leaders (Newborns, Crib, Toddlers and Walkers) and the Lord increases the ministry threefold, what do we do? Relax! We no longer need to stress or burn the midnight oil of worry. In the fractal design, the leader of the newborns finds four other leaders, and they each do the very same thing! Each chooses four new leaders with similar passions and supportive gifts to form another level of leadership. Growth is downward.

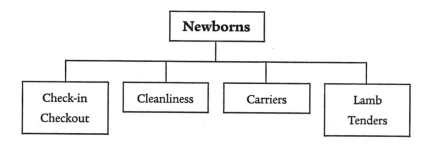

This can go on indefinitely, and you can get as creative as needed. In this way, every person is included, and every person has a role to fill. But remember, regardless of how large the ministry grows, God will always provide the servants necessary for the assignment.

GROWTH WITHOUT BURNOUT

Here's another wonderful aspect of this design. As the leader of children's ministry, I will primarily serve with four other leaders: the nursery and toddler leader, the prekindergarten and kindergarten leader, the first and second grade leader, and the third and fourth grade leader. These four people make up my team. But what happens when the ministry grows? How many leaders will I personally oversee?

Four.

What if the ministry doubles and we have to increase our leadership base by two more levels? How many people will I personally oversee if the ministry grows from 10 nursery-age children to 100?

Four.

What if it grows to 200?

Still four.

That's right. The answer will always be four! Each leader will always be overseeing four others. This way, no one burns out! You care for four people (or a team of five—yourself included, of course).

You see, at New Hope, growth is always downward. The larger the ministry, the deeper the leadership base goes.

NATURAL DISCIPLESHIP GROUPINGS

Another aspect of the genius of this design is that each team falls into natural groupings of five. These can become discipleship groups, each formed because of similar passions and paths of ministry. This may be the easiest and simplest way to begin a small-groups ministry at your church!

By seeing your leaders as your small group, then the common tasks become much more than a responsibility to be fulfilled. Each person can be individually cared for and nurtured by the group leader. Likewise, each of the four leaders will have their own groups of four. In this way, each person is being nurtured while they themselves are nurturing four others.

With the fractal design, our church becomes not a church with small groups but a church *of* small groups. Here, people are accountable to a leader, and that leader is accountable as well. Each person is discipling others as well as being discipled themselves.

SIMPLIFYING THE DESIGN

As we were taught in math class, I like to boil everything down to its lowest common denominator. I understand everything more clearly when it's in its simplest form, so that's what we did at New Hope. Using the principles of fractal leadership, we simplified the form so that we could teach it to our teams. Learning this one idea is foundational to everything we do.

Whether you are beginning a new ministry or taking part in an existing one, understanding the team-building process will certainly be helpful. I like to use pictures, so here's how I personally present the fractal design.

Step One
The first step in building your team, whether you're starting a new ministry or building another level into an existing one, is always the same. Begin by drawing a circle.

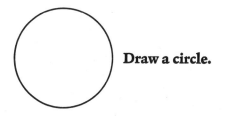

Draw a circle.

That's it. Simply draw a circle. This circle represents the parameters of your ministry. In concept, this is everything you will be responsible for.

If you are overseeing children's ministry, this circle embraces everything that is connected to that ministry. If you are a senior pastor, this represents everything about your church and its ministry: the services, pastoral care, leadership, counseling, discipleship, finances, organization, facilities and more—in other words, everything! If you are a volunteer overseeing the ushering ministry, this would include the passing out of bulletins, seating people and seeing to their needs. If you are a volunteer who directs the hospitality ministry, this circle will represent everything that the hospitality ministry includes, whether known or as yet unknown to you.

That's right. At this point, you may not know all that is contained within this circle. But don't worry. You'll discover its contents along the way. This simply sets the parameters, or boundaries, of your role.

Step Two
The second step is to draw a cross in the middle of the circle. Picture it as if you were looking through the viewfinder of a camera. The circle should now resemble the crosshairs in the lens. This shows you what you are aiming at, and that is exactly what this step is for.

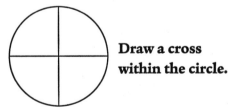

Draw a cross within the circle.

Now write down the purpose for your ministry. What is its intention, the God-glorifying purpose for what you are doing? Each ministry within the church should know its purpose with clarity and precision. Keep in mind the heart of the Great Commission along with the church's overarching mission statement. Then, in one or two sentences, articulate why you are embarking on this venture.

What is the goal of this ministry? What should it accomplish that will put this ministry in sync with the overall direction of the church?

Here are a few mission statements, or aims, at New Hope:

Front Lines Ministries

To present the gospel to non-Christians and Christians alike with simplicity and excellence. With the Holy Spirit's direction, we will redeem the arts for the glory of God and present the gospel in contemporary ways that will reach the heart.

Midweek LEAD Services

To develop mature, fruitful, soul-winning leaders.

New Hope Resources Ministry

The purpose of New Hope Resources is to be a source of supply and support that builds up the Body of Christ within, and to provide tools to reach out for the furtherance of the Great Commission.

Missions

Extending the heart of New Hope beyond Hawaii's borders for evangelism and bridge building.

Graphic Arts Ministry

Equipping the church with excellent and effective visual tools for communicating the gospel of Jesus Christ.

This step is crucial in doing church as a team. It gives everyone the same starting point for understanding how it all fits together. Without this step, individuals and individual ministries will be building from different sets of blueprints. Then, regardless of how sincere or how hard each one is trying, there will inevitably be colliding expectations.

Some ministries spend more of their time putting out personality fires than in doing the ministry. Why? Because they were inadvertently aiming at different targets. Their purpose must be identified up front. The clearer the target, the better the chance of hitting it!

Step Three
The next step begins by asking these questions:

- If this ministry (or project or responsibility) were broken into four separate quadrants, what would they be?
- What would I call each one?
- Would the combination of these four encapsulate the total responsibilities for fulfilling this ministry?

Title each quadrant of your circle with a heading that describes its purpose. The combination of these four should match the purpose statement you have just written. Likewise, your purpose statement should be in alignment with the overall statement of purpose for the church. (At the end of this chapter, the study guide will help you to practice these steps.)

New Hope Christian Fellowship's circle that encompasses the whole ministry looks something like this:

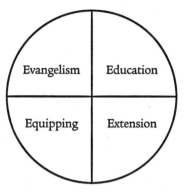

Step Four

The fourth step is to determine what gifts or gift mix would make the best fit for a person overseeing each quadrant. Would the gift of evangelism be necessary for someone serving as a leader in outreach events? Absolutely.

What about temperament? Would this person need to be primarily a task-oriented individual or more of a people-oriented person? Would this person best fit the task if he or she were an introvert? An extrovert?

All aspects of a person's DESIGN should be taken into consideration to find the best possible fit.

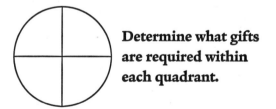

Determine what gifts are required within each quadrant.

Let's take a look at the distinction between an introvert and an extrovert for a moment.

An extrovert loves people, and when he is with people, they charge his batteries. When he is isolated from others, his batteries are drained. An introvert also loves people; however, when he is with people, they have a tendency to drain his batteries. He has to isolate himself periodically to recharge them.

Although I tend to be an introvert, I share many qualities with extroverts. I do need time alone to recharge my batteries, but when I am with people, my batteries drain very slowly. And if I am isolated for an extended length of time, I go stir crazy.

I remember when I was in the sixth grade, we were living in Japan. The winters were bitter cold. I attended a small military school in a town called Sagamihara. Miss Anne Clifford was the sixth-grade teacher. She was as tall as the school flagpole and as mean as they come. Believe it or not, from time to time, I would get disciplined by the teacher (for some silly, unfair and concocted reason, I'm sure). Her method of discipline was to confine me to the coat closet for 15 minutes per trumped-up charge.

Sitting in the dark for the first five minutes was tolerable, but at that point in my incarceration, I'd start to go crazy. I would rather she had tortured me with bamboo splinters under my fingernails. When I couldn't stand it any longer, I'd begin pacing the floor, counting the number of boards it took from one end to the other. Next I would try on all the coats, scrounge through the pockets for any leftover candies or switch one kid's boots with another kid's coat, making new and curious combinations.

You see, my temperament is such that I have to be with people. I hate being cooped up alone. I have to fellowship, talk and be with others.

In the same way, God knows your design, and He wants to match your internal makeup with your ministry, your temperament with your tasks. God knew my design, and that's the reason I am the way I am. If you don't like the way I am, don't blame me. It's God's fault! (You may laugh here.)

Step Five

In this step, identify the available people who possibly fit the required gift combinations. Ask yourself who in your congregation would be the best for the job. Talk to those who may know or who may have seen these different individuals in action. Do your best to fit the names with the gifts required, temperament needed and maturity necessary for the task or position in question. When this step is completed well, the chances are greater for each chosen leader to have a lasting and fruitful experience in ministry.

Step Six

The final step in slotting new and emerging leaders is to *ask*. Don't wait for volunteers to somehow magically appear uniformed and ready for duty. Challenge the men and women you think would fit. Because you've already done the research, many of those asked may be excited to sign up!

God has someone for each ministry He initiates, so don't force wrong pieces into slots by not doing your homework first. Guard yourself from the tendency to simply fill a position with a warm body. Follow the process; it will spare you many pains later on.

But ask, especially if you genuinely feel that you may release someone's dream! It is astonishing what you can accomplish simply by asking. Not only will you often receive what you ask for, but also many times the other person will thank you for taking the initiative!

Jesus did that. He asked. He found some potential disciples and asked each of them saying, "Come, follow me" (Mark 1:17, *NIV*). Jesus further instructs us to ask the Father for what we need: "Ask, and it shall be given to you; seek, and you shall find; knock, and it shall be opened to you" (Matt. 7:7).

One reason we may shy away from asking is fear. We worry about the outcome. We are concerned about offending or bothering people or that they might perceive us as needy or weak. Perhaps worse, they might perceive us as attempting to take advantage of our relationship with them. Relax! On the contrary, it is actually quite arrogant and self-righteous to assume that others aren't willing to help or assist. They may just be waiting to be asked!

Here's a key to asking someone to join up. You must be completely authentic in your invitation. You must be genuinely sincere in your belief that you want to see that person grow and be used in wonderful ways by the Holy Spirit!

A final reminder as we close this chapter: I am sure that you are a nice person and very capable but, quite frankly, you *need* people in ministry. You cannot develop the perfect ministry on your own. You cannot come up with all the creative ideas yourself. There are plenty of others who are as gifted, if not more so, than you! And there are plenty of others willing to pitch in and offer their expertise, advice and assistance.

When I get together with some of our staff and we gang up to tackle a problem, there's nothing we can't solve! Moreover, they spark all kinds of new ideas in me, and my creative juices start to overflow!

Note

1. *Merriam-Webster's Collegiate Dictionary*, 10th ed., s.v. "fractal."

CHAPTER NINE STUDY GUIDE

Practice building a team by following each of these steps:

1. What is the first step?

2. Next, draw the circle with crosshairs in it. What do the crosshairs represent?

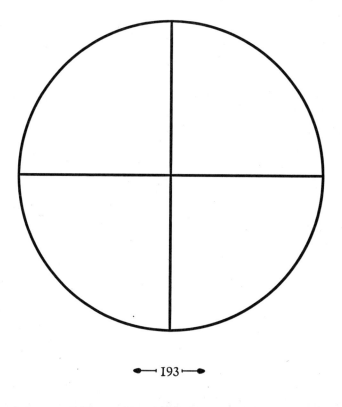

Write out the aim or purpose of the team you are building.

3. Next, title your four quadrants.

   a. Quadrant one:

   b. Quadrant two:

   c. Quadrant three:

   d. Quadrant four:

4. List the gifts necessary for being a leader in each quadrant.

   a.

   b.

   c.

   d.

5. Write the names of possible leaders for each of these quadrants.

   a.

   b.

   c.

   d.

6. Are you an introvert or an extrovert? On the continuum below, place an X where you think you fall.

Extreme   **Extreme**
Introvert   **Mild**   **Extrovert**

$\longleftarrow$ ——————————$\mid$—————————— $\longrightarrow$

0

7. Covering up the graph above, ask a friend or spouse to place an X on the graph below where they believe you fall.

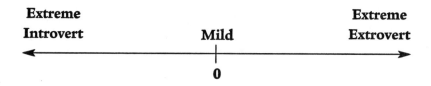

Extreme   **Extreme**
Introvert   **Mild**   **Extrovert**

$\longleftarrow$ ——————————$\mid$—————————— $\longrightarrow$

0

NURTURING THE TEAM

One of the highest of human duties is the duty of encouragement. There is a regulation of the Royal Navy which says: "No officer shall speak discouragingly to another officer in the discharge of his duties."

WILLIAM BARCLAY
SCOTTISH THEOLOGIAN
1907-1978

I HAVE THREE CHILDREN. OVER THE YEARS I HAVE WATCHED THEM GROW IN HEIGHT AS WELL AS IN MATURITY. ONE OBVIOUS THING I HAVE NOTICED ABOUT GROWTH: YOU DON'T HAVE TO FORCE IT OR PLEAD WITH IT TO HAPPEN. IT DOES SO ON ITS OWN! IF THERE IS A HEALTHY ATMOSPHERE AND THE FOOD IS NUTRITIOUS, BARRING THE INTRUSION OF ANY LIFE-THREATENING DISEASE OR ACCIDENT, GROWTH IS A NATURAL THING. IN FACT, IF EVERYTHING IS FAIRLY HEALTHY AND GROWTH IS NOT OCCURRING, THEN I GET WORRIED!

Churches are designed to be greenhouses for budding leaders with potential dreams in their hearts. Creating an atmosphere of health is one of the simplest, yet most overlooked, factors in growing healthy people and healthy leaders.

LIVING TO MAKE OTHERS SUCCESSFUL

In doing church as a team, we, as leaders, live to make the others in our team successful, not vice versa! If each member of the team is healthy and fulfilled, then the ministry benefits. If they are successful, people will be helped. It is absolutely necessary for each leader to cultivate a selfless spirit and live to make the other person successful.

That's exactly how the human body works. My lungs cheer for my heart to be healthy and to work well. Why? Not only for the heart's sake but also for the lungs' sake! You see, if the heart goes down, my lungs do, too. My stomach wants my kidneys to function well, and it also wants the liver to be in top form. Not only for their sake, but also for its own sake.

As a pastor, I need everyone in my church to be functioning well. This is not only for their sake but also for my good health! You see, if the setup crew doesn't function well, come Sunday morning, I am in trouble! If the Front Lines Team drops out or is dealing with internal struggles, it affects everything else in the Sunday services. What if the children's ministry falters? It throws everything else off kilter! It is absolutely critical that all the members be healthy, so everyone else will be healthy as well.

We live to make each other successful. That's the deal.

STEWARDING YOUR AUTHORITY WELL

For this reason I am writing these things while absent, in order that when present I may not use severity, in accordance with the authority which the Lord gave me, *for building up and not for tearing down* (2 Cor. 13:10, emphasis added).

Paul explains the purpose for authority. It is for building people up, not for tearing them down! Accepting and practicing this one truth will transform your people skills. God has no problem giving us authority if we will use it for His purpose—to build people up! Authority is a gift that puts you in a position to encourage others and bring out the best in people; it's not a tool for leveraging people in order to fulfill our desires.

When I was just starting off in the ministry, I was asked to sing at one of our denomination's conventions. Being a novice as well as a young Christian, it took all I had just to stand in front of this dignified group of pastors and leaders. I was so nervous that as my time to sing approached, all the water drained out of my mouth and into my hands.

I stood in front of nearly 700 pastors and after I gave a short testimony, I began my solo. Nervousness gripped my shaky song and flattened all the high notes. My mind went blank on the second verse, so I made one up as I went along. It was horrible. I prayed secretly that the Lord would come and rapture me before the song ended.

Finally, the ordeal came to a close. I made a secret vow to myself that as soon as the main speaker finished, I was going to grab my guitar and leave—not just the conference, but Bible college as well. I thought, *If I can't stand up and share with other convinced Christians, how will I ever be able to stand as a pastor in front of non-Christians! What a sham I am!* But as I lunged for my guitar to leave, the president of the denomination motioned to me, and he asked me to sit down with him.

Thoughts of despair ran through my mind. I was history! I knew I was about to be expelled or maybe, if I was fortunate, just reprimanded. I had no idea what this man was about to say.

He looked deeply at me for a moment, and then he began. Because of his authority and my deep respect for him, his words were indelibly etched into my soul.

He said, "Wayne, I know you were nervous tonight." I didn't tell him that I had made up one whole verse! He continued, "But I want you to know how impressed I was by your sincerity. I watched you win a decisive battle tonight. You conquered your nervousness because you wanted to exalt the Lord more than anything else in the world! And it showed. Sometimes I want to quit. I make a mistake and I beat myself to death because of it. But from now on, when I want to quit, I will remember you and your stalwart stand tonight. You see, courage isn't the absence of fear; it is pressing on in spite of it! God has His hand on you, and because you want to please Him, He will use you in wonderful ways. He has great things in store for you. Keep singing. Keep speaking to people of His great love."

I could have floated out of the convention hall that evening! Those simple but sincere words impacted me tremendously. During the next three years, I recorded my first album of original songs, traveled each summer for the Bible college (which paid for my tuition and room and board) and joined Youth For Christ as a youth evangelist! Much of what I am today is because of one person who stewarded well his authority and took the time to encourage a wet-behind-the-ears Bible school student.

Sure, one of my friends could have encouraged me by saying "Great job!" and giving me a pat on the back. That would have been nice. But when someone in authority uses an encouraging word to build you up, you can run on that for years!

Do you want more authority? Start building people up! It's just that simple. When God sees that you are willing to use whatever authority you have to encourage the best in others, He will give you more. My prayer is that our churches will be filled with great authority, as we see God's people realizing their dreams and being all they can be for the King!

THE THREE C'S OF HEALTHY CHURCHES

Let me give you the three C's of a healthy church atmosphere. I learned this at one of Bill Hybels's seminars on leadership. Bill and his wonderful staff at Willow Creek Association are unselfish servants with a desire to see local churches everywhere increase in fruitfulness.

Cause

The first C stands for the *cause* behind the church, or why the church exists. Cause is to a church what an engine is to an automobile—it is that which drives its passion and activities. Cause gives people motivation to overcome the hills and valleys every ministry encounters along the way. It is the bottom line by which all else can be measured.

May I be so bold to suggest that this cause is evangelism? Without lost people coming to a saving knowledge of Jesus Christ, all our efforts are in vain. We might have wonderful Bible studies, great potlucks, outstanding small groups and magnificent Sunday services. But unless people are giving their hearts to Jesus, what do all our activities amount to?

Granted, discipleship and Bible studies are critical to building people, but this should never be to the exclusion of winning the lost!

I often remind those at New Hope of the reason for our weekend services. We don't have Sunday services to maintain and entertain the convinced. As I have already mentioned, our weekend services allow us to "partner with each member in their attempts to reach their friends and family for Christ." We have a heart for the lost.

The cause for why we exist as a church must never be compromised or deprioritized. On a scale of one to ten, this should be bouncing up above the eight mark. Nothing adds excitement and an atmosphere of celebration to a church like a consistent inflow of new believers! If people are not coming to know Christ, we should immediately rethink what we are doing and retool!

Let me take you back for a moment to our statement of purpose. If you recall, it states that New Hope exists "to present the gospel in such a way that turns non-Christian into converts." Therefore, if people are not coming to know Christ as their Lord and Savior, then we are not presenting the gospel effectively.

The gospel never changes, but cultures do. Therefore, our style must accurately address the culture to which we've been called. This includes our music, facilities, parking, greeters, ambiance, activities—everything! Yes, everything matters when it comes to reaching people with the gospel of Christ. Whether or not they can understand the gospel in a way that results in their giving their hearts to Jesus is of utmost importance to us. Whatever must be recalibrated so that this happens, we will do it!

The cause of evangelism must always remain strong.

Community

A second factor found in healthy churches is a sense of *community*. The word depicts the free interchange, open fellowship and genuine relationships that glue people together. It has little to do with programs or activities but has much more to do with what happens between people *during* these programs or activities.

In John's first epistle, we find him alluding to this principle of community: "If we walk in the light as He Himself is in the light, we have fellowship with one another, and the blood of Jesus His Son cleanses us from all sin" (1 John 1:7). This fellowship is what binds people together. It is this sense of community that brings depth to a congregation, adds life to activities and turns a crowd into a family. This is where life is found. No matter how many gatherings, ministries, projects or concerts a church organizes, without *life* present within each one, the activity is useless.

Community is the life, the gel that fuses hearts together. In the absence of community, a church might easily become a high-octane, crusade-driven ministry, or it can fall victim to entropy and end up becoming keepers of traditions (see Mark 7:9).

Some years ago in Hilo when we were in the middle of our building program, we purchased a 20-acre lot; and after a few years, we raised enough money to begin building. I recall the day we poured the cement for our fellowship hall. It was an area larger than that of a high-school gymnasium, so this was no small task!

Fifty men gathered at early dawn on a Saturday. We each wore a pair of rubber boots and the oldest, most disposable clothes we could find. The trucks began arriving at 7 A.M. The sun rose like a golden disk, watery at first, but then it began burning our skin as the morning wore on. Beads of sweat rolled off our foreheads only to be mixed into the concrete. We ate a late lunch provided by the ladies from the church, as the cement cured under the midafternoon sun. After completing the project, we kicked off our boots and sat in huddles, summarizing the events of the day. We laughed, chided each other and relived every minute of the pour, over and over and over again. By the time we had washed our trowels and headed for home, it was dark.

Looking back on that day, the most endearing memories I have are not of the pour itself but, rather, what happened between our hearts during the pour. We arrived as brothers in Christ, and by the end of the day, we left not only as brothers but also as friends. The pour was not an end in itself but a means of achieving something much more eternal.

It's called life.

Community happens where there's a sense of
celebration and relationship.

Community happens when there's a sense of celebration and relationship, regardless of the activity. It happens when each gathering takes on the atmosphere of a family reunion, where hugs are abundant and bursts of laughter come easily. It happens when people enjoy just being with one another and where the atmosphere is more than just friendly.

A recent study found that when people visit a church, they are not just looking for friendly people; they are looking for friends. They need to sense in you a genuine willingness to open your life and let another in. Cultivate and guard this quality in your life and in your church.

Corporate
The third quality of a healthy church is healthy *corporate* finances—not necessarily abundant finance but the wise stewardship of what is there. Paying the rent, turning on lights and staying current with the monthly bills all require adequate finances and good stewardship.

The area of stewardship is more important than most leaders realize. Jesus says in Luke 16:11, "If therefore you have not been faithful in the use of unrighteous mammon, who will entrust the true riches to you?" The way Jesus sees it, the way we handle finances as a church will determine whether we will be faithful with "true riches." Whether those true riches be influence, spiritual gifts or authority, our stewardship over what He has given us is like a boot camp for things eternal.

All three of these C's need to be vigilantly monitored. When one or more of these begin to slump, energy and action should be expended to immediately remedy the situation.

A FINAL WORD

There is so much yet to be learned. I am still writing this book. As time goes on, I plan to add to it. Often I feel as if I am in the kindergarten stage of learning how to shepherd God's people and build leaders who will catch the heart and vision of Jesus Christ for the lost. This world is crying out for godly leaders who have allowed the Holy Spirit to develop within them a spirit of excellence and an ongoing desire to receive advice and remain teachable.

I love what God is beginning to do in the churches. There is a new wine being poured out, and only hearts made of new wineskins will be able to survive the pour! The others will burst and spill their contents, remaining ornate but empty wineskins.

Some time ago, I went out to a movie. The story line was magnificent. During the two hours or so that I watched, a tapestry of people and events was spun before my eyes. It was a wonderful experience.

On the way out, being a curious sort of person who loves to see how things work, I walked up a short flight of stairs and poked my nose into the projection booth. The film that captured the wonderful story I had just experienced was contained on a large, round platter. There must have been a mile or two of film, with each frame holding a tiny portion of the story in its celluloid embrace.

The light rays of the projector had cast its beam onto the screen while frame after frame rolled steadily before it. Frame after frame after frame. The quick but steady pace of the frames passing gives the images the illusion of moving; hence, the inaugural name of the "moving picture" shows, as they were called during my grandfather's days.

Suppose you stopped one of the frames and held it still before the projector lens. You would see an image in suspended animation (just before the film melted from the intense heat of the xenon lamp). Seeing that one frame alone without the rest of the frames marching in cadence before the light's beam wouldn't give you much understanding of the movie. You need that one frame moving in sequence with the many other frames in order to understand the whole story.

Every one of us is like a single frame in God's story, and each frame is incredibly important to God's plan. How often we think that no one would miss us if we didn't show up! If a bunch of frames decided to go on strike and walk out of the film, we would be hard pressed to make any sense of the movie. And we can do that as Christians. Justifying our inaction by our tiny, insignificant existence, we simply choose not to get involved. When that happens, no wonder the world's picture of the Church is jumpy and jerky!

But if we are serious about presenting a clear picture of the Lord to a desperate world, then we must each take our place. Be faithful in the frame that God has allotted to your care. Develop it with color! Then plug into the cadence of those with whom He has called you.

And as we do church as a team, you watch. You wait. You'll see one of the most beautiful and moving pictures of the heart of Jesus unfold right before your eyes.

Ho`omakaukau? I mua!

Ready? Paddle forward!

CHAPTER TEN STUDY GUIDE

1. What are the three C's of church health? What does each C stand for?

   C _____

   C _____

   C _____

2. If you are a pastor, use a scale of one to ten to rate each C in your church based on where you feel it currently ranks. List at least three ways the church can increase its effectiveness in each area.

   C _____ Rank _____

       a. _____

       b. _____

       c. _____

C_____ Rank _____

    a. _____

    b. _____

    c. _____

C_____ Rank _____

    a. _____

    b. _____

    c. _____

3. I will commit to the following changes in my thinking:

I will commit to the following changes in my ministry:

4. You are a 10 ... somewhere! Where are you currently serving?

If you are not, where do you plan to become involved?

5. Take a few minutes to write a note to your pastor and let him know of your support. If you are a pastor, take time right now to send a note of appreciation to your key leaders, thanking them for partnering with you in doing church as a team.

WAYNE CORDEIRO

is senior pastor of New Hope Christian Fellowship in Oahu, a new work that was planted in September 1995. Within five years, attendance at their weekend services had grown to more than 7,000, making New Hope Oahu one of the fastest growing churches in America. More than 5,200 people received Christ for the first time during these first years of the church.

Pastor Wayne has also planted more than twenty other churches in Hawaii, Guam, Samoa, Finland and Japan. Prior to moving to Oahu, he was senior pastor at New Hope Christian Fellowship in Hilo, Hawaii, for almost 12 years. Under his pastoral leadership, the New Hope Hilo congregation grew from 50 to over 1,700 and launched a new 20-acre church facility, The Gathering Place.

Wayne was raised in Palolo Valley on Oahu, and he lived in Japan for three years. He then moved to Oregon where he finished his schooling and ministry training during the next 12 years. He served with Youth For Christ for seven years and as a staff pastor for three years at Faith Center Foursquare Church in Eugene, Oregon, before returning to Hawaii.

He is an accomplished songwriter and performer who has released six albums. Pastor Wayne's teaching radio program, "Words of New Hope," airs on KAIM and KUMU in Hawaii. As president of the Pacific Rim Bible Institute, he is working to train, develop and support emerging leaders who will plant twenty-first-century churches in the Pacific Rim.

Pastor Wayne travels extensively throughout the islands, the continental United States and Asia to speak at conferences, churches, civic gatherings, prisons, high school assemblies, business forums and leadership conventions. He also speaks to businesses, companies and corporations about restructuring and growth strategies.

He has written four books: *Doing Church as a Team*, *Gems Along The Way*, *Developing an Attitude That Attracts Success* and the forthcoming Regal book *The Dream Releasers*.

Pastor Wayne and his wife, Anna, have three children, Amy, Aaron and Abigail.

For more information about resources by Wayne Cordeiro or to inquire about speaking engagements, please write or call:

NEW HOPE CHRISTIAN FELLOWSHIP OAHU

290 Sand Island Road
Honolulu, Hawaii 96819
Phone (808) 842-4242
Fax (808) 842-4241
www.eNewHope.org

New Hope International

M I N I S T R I E S

Wayne Cordeiro is the president of New Hope International. NHI is a ministry dedicated to identifying, equipping and sending emerging leaders to plant 21st century churches in the Pacific Rim, as well as a church consulting and training group which hosts leadership practicums and seminars for pastors. It also sponsors restructuring and church consulting teams which assist ministries in increasing their fruitfulness.

ELI ministries (Emerging Leaders International) is a scholarship program to support young leaders training for ministry. If you are interested in more information on becoming an ELI partner, please call or write us at the address below.

Leave your greatest legacy today by sponsoring an emerging leader who may change a nation tomorrow!

NEW HOPE INTERNATIONAL
290 Sand Island Access Road
Honolulu, HI 96819
NHI@eNewHope.org
808-842-4242

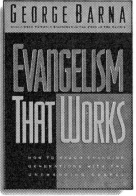
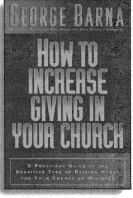
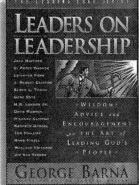

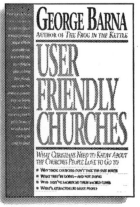
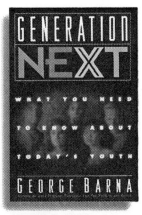